Broadway Christian Church Fort Wayne
Stop Dating the Church Fall In Love wi...   CL01 Har
Harris, Joshua

0000 4857   P9-CCV-052

"Instead of asking what they can give or how they can serve, too many churchgoers are only interested in what they can get. The church deserves far more than the halfhearted commitment or apathetic neglect it so often receives. In fact, as Harris astutely observes, the Christian life can never be lived to its fullest apart from a genuine passion for the church. It's time for believers to take the church seriously, which is why the message of this book is so essential."

—JOHN MACARTHUR

"Evangelical Christians have a good and appropriate emphasis on personal salvation. But that emphasis has not been balanced by the inherently corporate nature of the Christian life. Christians belong in churches—the only places where we can thrive and grow spiritually. In this book, Joshua Harris makes this case with wisdom, clarity, and graciousness."

—CHARLES W. COLSON
PRISON FELLOWSHIP, WASHINGTON, DC

"Joshua Harris reminds us of the great kingdom work we are missing in our lives when we avoid the personal contact that commitment to a 'home' church brings. Many people seek to be comfortable and well fed in a church, but community is where the real issues of our hearts get worked out. Through the church, Joshua Harris writes, 'The power of the gospel is not only changing individuals, but is also creating a whole new kind of humanity.'"

—SARA GROVES, SINGER/SONGWRITER

"Joshua Harris has a gift for addressing issues that matter in a way that's clear, powerful, and memorable. *Stop Dating the Church!* is the same kind of writing Josh's readers have come to expect and love—he's right and he's real. He winsomely shows the fallacy of those who want a relationship with Jesus, but not a committed relationship with His people. I believe the Lord will use this book to kindle in the hearts of many a love for what Jesus loves—His bride, the church."

—DONALD S. WHITNEY
AUTHOR OF *SPIRITUAL DISCIPLINES FOR THE CHRISTIAN LIFE*

"Pastors, are you looking for a good book to help visitors understand why they should join a church? Here it is! Clear, simple, well-illustrated, and compelling. This little book reflects Christ's love for the church and explains it in terms that are simple and passionate. Read it and use it."

—MARK DEVER, PASTOR OF CAPITOL HILL BAPTIST CHURCH
AND DIRECTOR OF 9 MARKS MINISTRIES

"In *Stop Dating the Church!* Joshua Harris passionately communicates the urgency of God's people becoming the counterculture we're called to be and gives us tools to get started. I appreciate that Josh has written this book with more than instruction; he writes it as one who also struggles with us to discover our own place in the body of Christ."

—DEREK WEBB, SINGER/SONGWRITER

STOP DATING THE CHURCH!

STOP DATING THE CHURCH!

JOSHUA HARRIS

Multnomah® Publishers *Sisters, Oregon*

STOP DATING THE CHURCH!
published by Multnomah Publishers, Inc.
© 2004 by Joshua Harris
International Standard Book Number: 1-59052-365-2

Cover design by David Carlson Design
Cover image by Conrad Damian Photography
Interior design and typeset by Katherine Lloyd, The DESK

Italics in Scripture are the author's emphasis.
Unless otherwise indicated, Scripture quotations are from:
The Holy Bible, English Standard Version © 2001 by Crossway Bibles,
a division of Good News Publishers. Used by permission. All rights reserved.

Other Scripture quotations are from: *The Holy Bible,* New International Version
(NIV) © 1973, 1984 by International Bible Society,
used by permission of Zondervan Publishing House

Multnomah is a trademark of Multnomah Publishers, Inc.,
and is registered in the U.S. Patent and Trademark Office.
The colophon is a trademark of Multnomah Publishers, Inc.

Printed in the United States of America

ALL RIGHTS RESERVED
No part of this publication may be reproduced, stored in a retrieval system,
or transmitted, in any form or by any means—electronic, mechanical,
photocopying, recording, or otherwise—without prior written permission.

For information:
MULTNOMAH PUBLISHERS, INC.
POST OFFICE BOX 1720 • SISTERS, OREGON 97759

Library of Congress Cataloging-in-Publication Data
Harris, Joshua.
  Stop dating the church! / Joshua Harris.
    p. cm.
  Includes bibliographical references.
  ISBN 1-59052-365-2
  1. Church. 2. Choice of church.   I. Title.
BV601.7.H37 2004
250--dc22

                                                          2004015520
04 05 06 07 08—10 9 8 7 6 5 4 3 2 1 0

To C. J.

CONTENTS

Chapter 1

CAN THIS RELATIONSHIP BE SAVED?

What We Miss When We Date the Church

J ack and Grace met through a mutual friend. From day one they seemed to be the perfect match. Grace was everything Jack had always wanted. She was beautiful, outgoing, and caring—always there when Jack needed her.

For the first five months they were inseparable. Jack could hardly think of anything but Grace. He didn't need to look further, he told friends. "She's the one."

Now almost three years have passed. Jack still enjoys

the comfort and familiarity of being with Grace, but the spark is gone. Grace's flaws seem more obvious. He's not sure he finds her as attractive as he once did. And he's beginning to resent all the time she wants to spend with him.

One night, when she asks if they can define the nature of their relationship, Jack blows up. "We're together, aren't we?" he asks angrily. "Why isn't that enough for you?"

Obviously, Jack isn't ready for commitment. And it's unclear if he ever will be….

Have you ever been in a relationship like this? I'm writing this book because I believe God has something better for you. He wants you in a relationship defined by both passion *and* commitment. But before you can take hold of this wonderful plan, you need to know something about this couple. There are millions of Jacks walking around today. And Grace isn't a girl.

Grace is a church.

Traveling Solo

This is my third book on relationships, but it's unlike any of my previous books. You won't find anything here about how you should relate to the opposite sex. Instead, this book is about how you should relate to the family of God.

The story behind this book is closely tied to my own

journey. I was raised in a Christian home, but even though the church played a big part in my life growing up, for many years it didn't have a big place in my heart.

My first home as a child was across the street from the little Baptist church my parents had gotten saved in during the Jesus Movement of the seventies. My dad was a pastor till I was seven and even planted a church in Texas. But after two disillusioning church splits, he left the pastorate and started speaking across the country on homeschooling. Over the years our family attended a wide spectrum of churches—mainline, evangelical, charismatic. One church gathered at a run-down commune complete with hippies and llamas. Another was a seeker-sensitive megachurch with a suburban campus that could pass for a shopping mall.

When I graduated from my church's high school youth group, I started visiting around. I loved God and had big dreams for how I wanted to serve Him, but I didn't see any reason to get too involved in one church. By then, I thought I knew all there was to know about church, and I wasn't impressed. Most churches struck me as out-of-date and out-of-touch. There had to be better, more efficient ways to accomplish great things for God.

For me, that meant becoming the next Billy Graham. But I was only nineteen, and invitations for me to lead a worldwide media crusade weren't rolling in. So I threw my energies into opportunities that were closer at hand. I started a magazine for homeschoolers. I began to speak at my own conferences for teenagers. Before long, I had written my first book, *I Kissed Dating Goodbye.*

The message of that book was that singles should avoid directionless relationships that were romantic and physical but had no intention of moving toward commitment. The irony of this was that even though I had stopped playing the dating game with girls, I was perfectly happy to keep playing it with the church. I liked attending on weekends, and I enjoyed the social benefits of church, but I didn't want the responsibility that came with real commitment. Like Jack in our story, I wasn't interested in settling down. So though I gave the appearance of commitment, I mostly just flirted with different churches and kept my options open.

Then something happened that I never expected.

A PASSIONATE ENCOUNTER

A friend sent me a set of sermons on tape called "Passion for the Church" by a pastor in Maryland. I'm still not sure why I listened to those tapes. For a confirmed church-dater like me, the title alone was baffling. "Passion for the church"? The words *passion* and *church* absolutely did *not* connect in my mind! The series might as well have been called "Passion for the Grocery Store." But for some reason, as I drove around my hometown of Gresham, Oregon, I popped those tapes into the cassette player and began to listen.

The preacher taught from the book of Ephesians. He showed that the church was actually God's idea—not some plan or program invented by humans. In fact, the church is the only institution God promised to sustain forever.

This is where passion came in. To be part of the universal church isn't enough, the preacher said. Every Christian is called to be passionately committed to a specific local church. Why? Because the local church is the key to spiritual health and growth for a Christian. And because as the visible "body of Christ" in the world, the local church is central to God's plan for every generation.

I have to tell you, the biblical truths in those messages picked me up, turned me over, and gave me a good shaking. Out of my pockets tumbled an avalanche of well-worn attitudes about the church. Most weren't carefully thought-out, it's true. But all of them were misguided, and some were unscriptural and dangerous. For the first time I realized that a wholehearted relationship with a local church is God's loving plan for me and for every other follower of Christ.

It is not just what my parents want for me. It is not just what some pastor thinks.

And it is not optional.

CAN YOU SPOT A CHURCH-DATER?

Today we live in an increasingly fragmented world. That mind-set has influenced the way we approach our relationship with God. Faith is a solo pursuit. These days, experts describe America as a nation of "believers" but not "belongers"—and the numbers confirm it. According to pollster George Barna, while the adult population in the United States increased by 15 percent during the nineties, the number of adults who either didn't attend church or only went on major holidays increased by 92 percent!

Can you spot what I'm calling a church-dater? Here's a quick profile. Do you see one or more of these characteristics in yourself?

First, our attitude toward church tends to be *me-centered*. We go for what we can get—social interaction, programs, or activities. The driving question is, "What can church do for me?"

A second sign of a church-dater is being *independent*.

We go to church because that's what Christians are supposed to do—but we're careful to avoid getting involved too much, especially with people. We don't pay much attention to God's larger purpose for us as a vital part in a specific church family. So we go through the motions without really investing ourselves.

Most essentially, a church-dater tends to be *critical*. We are short on allegiance and quick to find fault in our church. We treat church with a consumer mentality—looking for the best product for the price of our Sunday morning. As a result, we're fickle and not invested for the long-term, like a lover with a wandering eye, always on the hunt for something better.

Take my friend Nathan. He attended *two* churches on Sundays—one because he liked their music, the other because he liked the preaching. And his involvement in both went no deeper. At the first church he'd slip out just before the last song wound down and drive to the other church five minutes away. He even factored in time to stop by McDonald's for an Egg McMuffin. He timed it so that he'd be walking into the second church just as the pastor started to preach.

I guess you could say Nathan was two-timing.

If you see yourself in any of these descriptions, I want

you to hear this from a former church-dater: *God has something better for you and me than dating the church.* What practiced daters like Nathan and Jack don't realize is that what they assume is working for their personal gain is actually resulting in serious loss—for themselves and others.

I'm writing this book because I want to share with other sincere followers of Christ the profound blessings that come with living a life committed to the church. I want you to catch a glimpse of the beauty of God's plan for the church in each believer's life and the unimaginable power that could be unleashed through even one generation embracing that plan.

And why shouldn't that generation be ours?

But before we look at the benefits of commitment, consider what is lost when church dating becomes a way of life. The plain fact is, when we resist passion and commitment in our relationship with the church, *everyone* gets cheated out of God's best.

- You cheat *yourself.*
- You cheat a *church community.*
- You cheat your *world.*

I hope you have the courage to stay with me, because the biblical insights we're looking for in this book have the potential to bring tremendous change for the better in your life.

Let's start with the last idea. Your world.

YOUR LIFE IS BIGGER

Step back for a minute. Remember how high the stakes really are for every human life. Each of us lives out our earthly days in a visible world that just barely conceals a larger invisible reality. What we see won't last forever. We're in a cosmic conflict against the spiritual forces of evil (Ephesians 6:12). At some point in the future, every human being alive today will be dead, and there will be an accounting. Every one of the six billion souls on earth will spend eternity in either heaven or hell. That's why every human being alive today needs to hear the Good News of the gospel!

The Good News is simple and powerful—Jesus Christ died to save us from our sins, and there is no other way of salvation (see John 14:6; Romans 5:8). To receive the free gift of salvation Jesus offers, we must turn from our sin in genuine repentance and trust in Him and His sacrificial death on our behalf (see 1 John 1:8–9; Romans 10:9; Ephesians 2:8–9).

Have you heard this Good News before? Have you

responded to it and had your sins forgiven through faith in Christ? I hope so!

Now I want you to see how the church and the Good News connect: The church is the *vehicle* that Jesus chose to take the message of the gospel to every generation and people.

Are you seeing the bigger picture? The church matters because Jesus chose it to tell and show the world the message of His love. And this message, carried forward through history and lived out for all to see, is the world's *only* hope.

Paul David Tripp writes to Christians:

> Your life is much bigger than a good job, an understanding spouse, and non-delinquent kids. It is bigger than beautiful gardens, nice vacations, and fashionable clothes. In reality, you are part of something immense, something that began before you were born and will continue after you die. God is rescuing fallen humanity, transporting them into his kingdom, and progressively shaping them into his likeness—and he wants you to be a part of it.

Isn't this amazing? God has not only saved us; He has invited us to participate in His master plan of redeeming a people for His glory. Through the local church we take part in His eternal plan to rescue men and women from their sin and totally transform their lives. This is the mission of the church. It's our duty, our calling, and our privilege.

But as you'll see in the pages ahead, another powerful dimension is at work when we decide to take our role in the family of God seriously. As we become genuinely involved in the church's work in the world, we put ourselves in the best possible place to allow God to do His work in *us*. That's because the church is the best context— God's greenhouse, if you will—for us to flourish spiritually. It's here that God grows us and conforms us to the image of His Son. (And when I say "the church is the best context," I'm *not* only talking about what happens in the pew, or prayer room, or anywhere else inside the walls of a worship facility.)

The church *community* is where we learn to love God and others; where we are strengthened and transformed by truth from the Word; where we're taught to pray, to worship, and to serve; where we can be most certain that we're investing our time and abilities for eternity; where we can grow in our roles as friends, sons and daughters, husbands and wives, fathers and mothers. The church is earth's single best place—God's specially *designed* place— to start over, to grow and to change for the glory of God.

That's why I tell people that when they stop dating the church, they're not just adding another item to a long spiritual to-do list. Instead, they're finally getting started on experiencing *all the other blessings* that Jesus promised to His followers as the fruits of the truly abundant life.

WHY SHOULD YOU KEEP READING?

In the rest of this book, we'll look at how God views the church and how seeing the church from His perspective can transform our attitude. We'll narrow our view to look at "the church down the street"—what keeps us from really committing to it, and what we can do about that. We'll also examine the lifestyle changes that take place when we make the church a priority, as well as the tangible benefits this change brings. And we'll talk about what to look for in a local church when you're ready to commit.

For some, I know, just the idea of committing (or recommitting) to a church stirs up unpleasant feelings and memories. You may think you're doing just fine on your own. Or you may have had a bad experience at church in the past. Perhaps you've seen a church torn apart by greed, arrogance, or a lack of moral integrity. Any talk of commitment makes you balk or want to run. You don't want to give your heart and have it broken again.

If this is where my book finds you, I understand your feelings…and I hope you'll keep reading! My prayer is that in the pages ahead you'll dare to dream again of what your place in the community of faith was meant to be. And more than dream, that you'll believe that God's loving, unchanging purpose for you is stronger than anyone else's sin.

I'll admit, the prospect of falling head over heels in love can feel very risky. But God is calling us to just that kind of wholehearted and deeply involved experience with His church. He feels this kind of passion.

And I'm not exaggerating. Because, as you're going to see in the next chapter, Jesus still calls us His bride.

Chapter 2

HE STILL CALLS
HER HIS BRIDE

*Seeing the Church
from Heaven's Perspective*

My face is sore from smiling. My heart is beating as though I just ran a hundred-yard dash. But I'm standing still. Trying to stand tall. Waiting.

And then, the music soars. A door at the back of the church auditorium opens. I catch a glimpse of white, and I begin to tremble.

This is the moment.

Every head turns. Necks crane. The congregation rises in unison.

There is Shannon, leaning on her father's arm. She

seems to glow. If only there were a pause button I could press to make this scene stand still—just long enough to try to take it in. I want to savor every second.

Today is my wedding day. My bride has just walked into view.

PICTURE THIS

The Bible uses many striking word pictures to describe the church. Each of these pictures, some of which we'll explore in this chapter, is packed with meaning about the church. But one word picture seems most striking of all. It helps us see not only God's purpose for us, the church, but the depth of His love and commitment to our well-being. Paul tells us that Christ views the church like a bridegroom sees his *bride*.

That Jesus calls the church His bride never had much meaning for me. That is, until my wedding day. I can't recall all my thoughts and emotions as I watched Shannon walk down the aisle. But in the midst of my elation, I distinctly remember being struck by the thought that I was being given the tiniest glimpse of how Christ feels about all of us, His followers.

The joyful anticipation...

The pure love…

The boundless hope…

My experience in those moments hinted at the passion Christ has for His church. The word picture came alive like never before. Jesus calls *you and me* His bride.

Since this is a book about our relationship with the local church, you might wonder where all this gushy love talk comes in. If you've been significantly involved in one or more churches in the past, you may feel in a rush to have me understand your experiences—wonderful, less than wonderful, or just plain awful.

But I want to take a risk with you. I want to help you look at your experiences from a fresh angle. In the next chapter we'll focus on the local church as most of us have encountered it (we'll call it the little *c* church). But first I want you to think about the big *C* Church. This Church is not about any one building or congregation or denominational tradition. It is the larger family of God around the world, made up of all those who have received the gift of salvation by grace alone through faith in Jesus.

And I want you to consider a mystery:

What does that one word—*bride*—tell us about the nature of Jesus' love for this greater Church?

A PROFOUND MYSTERY

In Ephesians 5:25–32, Paul instructs husbands to love their wives just like Christ loved the church. You've probably heard this passage read at a wedding. It's usually applied to the obligations of husbands to care for and love their wives. This application is right and wonderful, but these verses also reveal a lot about what Jesus thinks of His church and how He chooses to love us.

Try reading the familiar verses again from a new perspective. Instead of focusing on what husbands should do, look at what these verses tell us about what Jesus has done for us and will do for those who are joined to Him by faith:

> Husbands, love your wives, as Christ loved the church and gave himself up for her, that he might sanctify her, having cleansed her by the washing of water with the word, so that he might present the church to himself in splendor, without spot or wrinkle or any such thing, that she might be holy and without blemish. In the same way husbands should love their wives as their own bodies. He who loves his wife loves himself. For no one ever hated his own flesh, but nourishes and cherishes it, just as Christ does the church, because we are

members of his body. "Therefore a man shall leave his father and mother and hold fast to his wife, and the two shall become one flesh." This mystery is profound, and I am saying that it refers to Christ and the church. (Ephesians 5:25–32)

Obviously when this passage speaks of the church, it's talking about more than any one congregation. It's referring to the big *C*, or universal, Church. This is the living, breathing spiritual family we join—and that we're joined to—the moment we're saved and baptized (baptism being the outward symbol of our inward spiritual rebirth, Acts 2:38).

How much does Christ love the Church? According to this passage, He loves us so much that He gave Himself up for us. He laid down His very life to redeem us. And now He is continually at work to cleanse and prepare us for eternity.

Christ's love for His Church is not flighty—He is tender and patient. His love isn't fickle—He is committed. He intercedes on our behalf constantly before the Father. He nourishes, cherishes, sustains, protects.

Christ's love for us is so deep and His identification with us so real that He views us as His own body. In our union with Him, His life extends to us. That means that

when we are rejected, He is rejected. When we are persecuted, He is persecuted. When we rejoice, He does, too.

Now notice that the Ephesians passage above ends
with a reference to Genesis 2, which says that in marriage
a man and wife become one flesh. Then Paul tells us that
the Genesis passage actually refers to Christ and the
Church. What is he saying? Is it possible that God didn't
get His inspiration for loving the Church from marriage,
but that one reason God *created* marriage was to illustrate
His love for the Church?

I think so. No wonder Paul calls the metaphor of the
Church as the bride of Christ a *profound* mystery!

God invented romance and pursuit and the promise of
undying love between a man and a woman so that
throughout our lives we could catch a faint glimmer of the
intense love Christ has for those He died to save. What
passion He has for His Church! Even if you've never studied the Bible, you've heard the echoes of this amazing love
throughout your life. Every true love story has hinted at it.
Every groom weakened at the sight of his radiant bride has
whispered of it. Every faithful, committed, and loving
marriage has pointed to it. Each is an imperfect echo of the
perfect love song of heaven.

To Love What He Loves

My goal in this book is to help you get connected and committed to a solid local church. But before any of us can understand how to relate to the church down the street, we need to see the Church as God sees it. That's why I've taken the time to show you some implications of the Church's being the bride of Christ. You see, the strongest argument I know for why you and I should love and care about the Church is that Jesus does. The greatest motivation we could ever find for being passionately committed to the Church is that *Jesus* is passionately committed to the Church.

As Christians we're called to be imitators of God (Ephesians 5:1). We're to be conformed to the image of His Son (Romans 8:29). Can there be any question that part of being like Jesus is to love what He loves? Christians often speak of wanting God's heart for the poor or the lost. And these are good desires. But shouldn't we also want God's heart for the Church? If Jesus loves the Church, you and I should, too. It's that simple.

But why is this so difficult for so many of us? I mean, what comes to mind when *you* think of the Church?

Let's face it. Most of us probably don't picture a beautiful bride. Our view of the Church is distorted by negative experiences or our own wrong perceptions. We picture a particular building, a bickering denomination, a fraudulent televangelist, or some embarrassing scandal that hits the news. The Church isn't something we're particularly proud of or drawn to in our hearts.

But maybe all that would change if we looked at the Church from heaven's perspective.

WHAT THEY SEE

The Bible teaches in Ephesians 3:9–11 that the "rulers and authorities in the heavenly places" look down at God's work through the Church with amazement and wonder. They're in awe. They're glued to the action unfolding through the Church. Why? Because the "manifold wisdom" of God is being displayed, and the spiritual mystery hidden for ages past is being revealed through the Church.

What is this wisdom? It's the powerful effects of the gospel being worked out in real lives and real relationships. Ephesians tells us that through the gospel sinners are not only being reconciled to God; they're also being reconciled to *each other* in the church.

> Consequently, you are no longer foreigners and aliens, but fellow citizens with God's people and members of God's household. (2:19)

The heavenly beings look down at the Church, and they see an amazing *family*. The power of the gospel is not only changing individuals, but is also creating a whole new kind of humanity. In the midst of a strife-torn world—a world divided by gender, by race, by class, and by political ideology—the Church is a city set on a hill where people who once hated God and each other become God's children and members of *one* family.

This family expresses itself in practical, yet radical, ways.

Maureen, a white woman from my church, has a particular burden for racial reconciliation. She came of age in the tumultuous sixties, when her parents were heavily involved in the Civil Rights movement. She graduated from T. C. Williams High School—the school featured in the movie *Remember the Titans*. "The movie didn't come close to describing the horror of attending the school during that time in history," Maureen says. "I witnessed my share of incendiary racial conflict and bigotry. And because I made a point of befriending black students, people of both races senselessly persecuted me."

Maureen hoped in vain that relations would change. They didn't, and she encountered similar disappointments in college and at work. "'We shall overcome' was the popular chant," she says, "but it is unattainable without God."

Maureen became a Christian at age twenty-five. Not long after, she fell in love with her church. She's seen things happen there that can't take place anywhere else on earth. "I recognized that the Church was the only place where people of different races could find the forgiveness, acceptance, and trust necessary for deep friendship."

Today Maureen's best friend is Jamaican, and she sees her kids enjoying diverse friendships, too. "My son Michael's best friends from church come from three separate nations: Nigeria, Mexico, and the Philippines. None are Caucasian. They aren't even American! And amazingly, they all take this for granted. Race is of minor importance here. Our equal relationship to Christ makes us members of the same family."

Maureen has caught a glimpse of what heaven sees.

TWO MORE PICTURES

The Church of Jesus Christ is a family like no other. But the mystery doesn't end there. When heavenly beings look down, they also see something even more amazing—they see a *body*.

And God placed all things under his feet and appointed him to be head over everything for the church, *which is his body*, the fullness of him who fills everything in every way. (Ephesians 1:22–23, NIV)

The Church is so close to the heart of God, so central to His work in the world, that He calls us the *body* of Christ. We're more than brothers and sisters in Christ. As we express our union with Him through service, worship, and love, we become the physical manifestation of our Savior on the earth.

Ready for another word picture? Heaven sees the Church as a magnificent temple. Through the Church, God is creating a structure like no other in history. It's not made of stones or bricks. It's greater than any cathedral built with human hands. This building is composed of *living* stones (1 Peter 2:5). The apostles and prophets laid the foundation, Jesus Himself is the cornerstone, and you and I are being joined to it.

In him the whole building is joined together and rises to become a holy temple in the Lord. And in him you too are being built together to become a dwelling in which God lives by his Spirit. (Ephesians 2:21–22, NIV)

As believers, we are joined to a spiritual structure that links us to the apostles who walked with the Master, to the saints from every generation, color, and continent—both those that preceded us and those that will follow.

In the Old Testament, God's presence in the world was manifested in the tabernacle in the wilderness and later in the temple in Jerusalem. But today, after the coming of Christ, there is no need for a temple. The church is the temple of God—the place where He specially resides and manifests His presence. *We* are the dwelling of God, not our buildings, but our lives joined together in worship and service.

PUTTING IT ALL TOGETHER

Are you seeing more clearly why it's so important that we be connected and committed to the church?

Eric Lane describes what each of these pictures of the church says about our part in it:

> To be a member of a family is to belong to a community bound by a common fatherhood. To be a stone in his temple means to belong to a worshipping community. To be part of a body means

to belong to a living, functioning, serving, wit-
nessing community.

"Put together," Lane continues, "you have the main
functions of an individual Christian. Evidently we are
meant to fulfill these not on our own but together in the
church."

He's right. We can't live out our Christian lives on our
own. When we're saved from our sin, we become part of
something bigger than ourselves—a family, a body, a
temple. Through the Church around the world, God is at
work glorifying Himself and transforming lives.

This is the Church from all tribes and tongues and
generations that will be presented like a bride to Christ on
the last day (see Revelation 19:7).

This is the Church that will triumph in spite of human
failure and demonic attacks.

This is the Church that will never end.

THOSE PROMISING DIFFERENCES

By now you might be thinking that God's plan for the
church sounds great, but obviously it has fallen apart.
What about all those denominations? Aren't they evidence

that the unity Jesus prayed for in John 17 has not been achieved? Don't they prove that the church is a failed experiment? If you find yourself held back by these reservations, I encourage you to rethink the meaning of *unity*.

True unity is by the Spirit of God through faith in the gospel. Any form of unity that forsakes the central truths of the gospel—the substitutionary atonement of Christ, His resurrection, and justification by grace alone through faith alone—is no unity at all. All those who hold and cherish these core truths—the kind of truths that Paul described as of "first importance" (1 Corinthians 15:3–5)—enjoy true unity. We're one in Christ, even if we exist on opposite sides of the world and worship in different traditions.

So you don't have to think of denominational differences as the enemy of unity, but as something that makes true unity more achievable. We agree to agree on things of first importance; we agree to respect disagreements on things of lesser importance. "Denominations allow us to have organizational unity where we have full agreement," writes Richard Phillips, "and allow us to have spiritual unity with other denominations, since we are not forced to argue our way to perfect agreement but can accept our differences of opinion on secondary matters."

In the most important way, Jesus' prayer for unity

has been answered. Because of the gospel, there is unity. Our job is to maintain it. How do we do this? By rejecting a *denominational spirit* in our attitude. By praying for God to work through other Christians even though they might worship differently than we do. By being humble about doctrinal differences of secondary importance. And by rejoicing when we hear of others being used to advance the gospel.

When we embrace this attitude, we'll start seeing the Church around the world for the remarkable phenomenon that it is.

Jean recently moved to Egypt. One Sunday morning she was struck by the fact she was worshiping alongside brothers and sisters from over sixty countries. "We had gathered together, united in purpose, to glorify and worship Jesus Christ," she wrote me. "We were united under one Head. I got a glimpse of what heaven will be like— every tribe, language, and nation will be represented."

Through His Church, spread out around the world, Jesus is glorifying Himself and extending His reign in ways that no single person, congregation, or denomination could do alone.

TIME HAS NOT DIMMED HIS LOVE

When we see the church as God sees it, we learn two extremely important lessons. First, church matters to Him more than we realize. And second, He calls and expects us to be part of it…because we *are* part of it!

If Jesus loves the church, you and I should, too. We can't use the excuse that the church has messed up too many times or that we're disillusioned. Jesus is the only person who has the right to disown and give up on the church. But He never has. And He never will.

I met a man who had been married over twenty-five years. As he told me about himself and his family, he reached for his wallet. "Let me show you a picture of my bride," he said excitedly. I half expected to see a worn photo of his wife from their wedding day. Instead he handed me a recent picture of his wife, now in her fifties. I smiled in admiration. This man's obvious love for his wife was inspiring. She wasn't "the old lady" to him. Even the term *wife* didn't express all that was in his heart. After a quarter century of life together, she was still his bride. She still had his heart, his passion, and his affection.

The Bible tells us that Jesus has a similar and even greater affection for us, His Church. Despite all our missteps, sin, and imperfections, Christ's love for His Church hasn't changed over time. John Stott writes:

On earth she is often in rags and tatters, stained and ugly, despised and persecuted. But one day she will be seen for what she is, nothing less than the bride of Christ, "free from spots, wrinkles or any other disfigurement," holy and without blemish, beautiful and glorious. It is to this constructive end that Christ has been working and is continuing to work. The bride does not make herself presentable; it is the bridegroom who labours to beautify her in order to present her to himself.

Jesus is at work every day making us beautiful. He chose us before the foundation of the world (Ephesians 1:4–6). He had us in mind as He hung dying on the cross. So many days have passed since then. But His passion hasn't dimmed.

Jesus still calls us His bride.

Chapter 3

WHY WE REALLY NEED THE LOCAL CHURCH

Thinking Globally, Loving Locally

I met Michael at a bookstore near my home. Twenty-something and sporting a goatee, he had thick black hair that piled up and stood out in several directions. He was sprawled on one of four plump green chairs at the intersection of two aisles of books. What caught my attention about him was that in the midst of all those books he was intently reading a Bible. I struck up a conversation. He told me he was a Christian but was going through a difficult time in his life and faith.

Eventually I asked, "So where do you go to church?"

"I don't really," he said. He raked his hand through his

hair and sighed. "The last two churches I went to both went through nasty splits right after I showed up," he said. Then he laughed. "I'm convinced that I jinx churches."

When I invited Michael to visit my church, he asked, "Are you sure you want me and my bad luck?"

"I don't believe in luck," I told him. Michael did visit our church a few weeks later, but I haven't seen him since. Is he out there still trying to navigate his Christian journey alone, or has he joined a church fellowship? I'll probably never know.

Sadly, there are too many Michaels—uninterested, disillusioned, distrustful. "Most Christian young adults know what they believe," a girl named Holly told me. "And they think as long as they have that figured out, they don't need a church family or the things that go along with it. Besides, it's just a formality for Christians that isn't really necessary."

Is belonging to a church really just a formality? When asked what church she belonged to, one Sunday-morning visitor told a pastor, "The universal body of Christ."

Technically, she may be right. As we saw in the last chapter, every authentic Christian *does* belong to Christ— and that's wonderful! But is it either wise or right for a person to be linked spiritually to the universal Church yet have no connection to a local church? Is it even possible?

Wouldn't that be like telling your new bride that while your love is true, you have other priorities? Your heart of course is all hers, but as for the rest of you…well, you'll be in and out.

I propose that for sincere followers of Christ, the Bible allows no such disconnect. If you and I identify with and love the *idea* of church, we must consider how we can identify with and love an *actual* church.

THINK GLOBALLY, LOVE LOCALLY

A local church is a visible, tangible, real-world expression of the body of Christ. "Of course every believer is part of the universal church," writes Chuck Colson. "But for any Christian who has a choice in the matter, failure to cleave to a particular church is failure to obey Christ."

Charles Spurgeon agreed that for a Christian, failure to join a church is disobedience. He combined piercing truth and humor when he compared such disconnected Christians to "good-for-nothing" bricks:

> I know there are some who say, "Well, I have given myself to the Lord, but I do not intend to give myself to the church."
>
> Now why not?

"Because I can be a Christian without it."

Are you quite clear about that? You can be as good a Christian by disobedience to your Lord's commands as by being obedient?

What is a brick made for? To help build a house. It is of no use for that brick to tell you that it is just as good a brick while it is kicking about on the ground as it would be in the house. It is a good-for-nothing brick.

So you rolling-stone Christians, I do not believe that you are answering your purpose. You are living contrary to the life which Christ would have you live, and you are much to blame for the injury you do.

Only by joining a local church can Christians avoid "kicking about on the ground" like a brick. It's in the local church that we are attached to God's work around the world.

Authors Brian Habig and Les Newsom, in *The Enduring Community,* make a helpful recommendation. Borrowing from the bumper sticker, they recommend that Christians should "Think globally, love locally." "All of us should concern ourselves with the challenges that face all people everywhere," they write. "But that concern cannot be expressed everywhere. We demonstrate our concern by acting and living where we are."

We see this combination of a global mind-set with a local focus throughout the New Testament. The apostles weren't just caught up with the universal Church—they were busy planting and caring for individual local churches. Most of their epistles were written to specific churches in cities like Galatia, Ephesus, Corinth, and Philippi. Almost every time the word *church* appears in the New Testament it means a particular gathering of Christians.

They saw the big picture, but they understood that you could never separate God's big-picture plan from everyday service and involvement with people.

People like your neighbors, for example.

WHAT THE CHURCH DOES BEST

One thing a local congregation does best is to show your non-Christian neighbors that the *new life* made available through Jesus' death on the cross is also the foundation for a *new society*. By living the gospel as a distinct community, the church down the street accomplishes the important mission of displaying the transforming effects of the gospel for the world to see. Others won't be able to see this larger picture if we remain detached from each other and go our separate ways.

My wife, Shannon, first heard the gospel from her guitar teacher. Then, when he brought her to church, she saw the gospel in action. Here were hundreds of people who trusted in, worshiped, and lived for Jesus Christ. She started reading the Bible, then saw it being lived out in real life by real people. In the church she encountered people who cared for one another, who forgave one another, who served one another. It was different from anything she'd seen in her life. God used the combined witness of the church to bring her to personal faith in Christ.

If Christ did bring new life as He said, Christians should be living differently than non-Christians. Don't you agree? Of course, we don't always do this perfectly. But we should do everything possible to keep our light shining brightly in a dark world, on display for all to see. Part of the local church's job is to distinguish those who believe from those who don't—to show what it means to truly follow Christ. That's also why a local church must maintain certain uniquely Christian practices given us by Jesus.

Consider the distinctive ordinances a church is called to measure itself by:

- *Baptism* shows those who have been saved and who have identified with the death and resurrection of Christ (see Matthew 28:19; Romans 6:4).

- *The Lord's Supper* shows those who are continuing in fellowship with Christ and are remembering His death until His return (see Matthew 26:26–29; 1 Corinthians 11:23–25).

- *Discipline* is the process that removes a person from the church who is acting and living in ways that contradict New Testament teaching for godly living. In order to most helpfully love the person in unrepentant sin, and so as not to confuse others as to what it means to be a Christian, church leadership lovingly puts them out of the church in the hope they'll be restored (see Matthew 18 and 1 Corinthians 5:1–9).

You can see right away, then, that a local church is different from a campus ministry or a neighborhood Bible study. These groups can express many aspects of Christian community, but they are not church. Church is also more than just a group of Christians coming together for encouragement. It's more than listening to preaching on the radio or chatting on the phone with a Christian in another city.

Yes, you could get a teaching or fellowship "fix" in those contexts. But none of them can substitute for a local church that displays the distinct qualities of a God-honoring community. None can provide an individual believer with the leadership of a pastor or the care and encouragement of a many-textured, but mutually committed, church family.

Many aspects of our faith benefit from the involvement of others. Let's look at two other areas. The first is the lifelong pursuit of godliness. What we can do alone as Christians—while meaningful and indispensable—is no substitute for what can and does happen in the local church.

SANCTIFICATION IS A COMMUNITY PROJECT

The longer I'm a Christian, the more aware I become that I cannot live the Christian life on my own. My individual and direct relationship with God through Jesus is the greatest privilege and He is truly all I need—and yet God in His wisdom has created all of us to need others, too. Is this a contradiction? Not at all—for God has ordained that much of His grace flows to us *through others*. Says Pastor John Piper, "Sanctification is a community project."

In five verses in Hebrews 10, we see this two-fold path for the Christian clearly laid out. In verses 19–23, we're encouraged to draw close to God and relate to Him personally and intimately. We're invited to confidently "enter the holy places by the blood of Jesus"! It goes on to tell us to stand strong in our faith as believers, to "hold fast the confession of our hope without wavering, for he who promised is faithful."

What more do we need?

Evidently we do need something more. And in verses 24–25, we're told what it is:

> And let us consider how to stir up one another to love and good works, not neglecting to meet together, as is the habit of some, but encouraging one another, and all the more as you see the Day drawing near.

You see, we really do need the ministry of others—especially pastors—to encourage us, to help us apply God's Word to our lives and to help us see our sins.

Recently my wife and I got into an argument that escalated into anger on both our parts. We tried to resolve our differences several times, but each attempt only exacerbated the problem. I was at a loss. I wanted to resolve the conflict, but didn't know how.

The next morning I spent an hour praying and reading Scripture. I wrote my thoughts down in my journal. Nothing seemed to help. I still couldn't see my way out of the situation. So I picked up the phone and called my pastor. "You okay?" C. J. asked as soon as he heard my voice. I explained the situation and told him how confused I was. "Carolyn and I will be over tonight," he said. "Remember, there's no conflict you and Shannon can have that we haven't had."

C. J. and Carolyn arrived that night after our kids were in bed. We prayed together, and then they listened patiently as we recounted the argument. Though we spoke calmly and kindly, we were still focused on blaming each other. (As C. J. later put it, we did an outstanding job of confessing each other's sin!) Finally, C. J. and Carolyn gently interrupted us and pointed out the obvious bitterness in our hearts. They encouraged us to humble ourselves before God and deal with our bitterness before we tried to work out the specifics of our disagreement.

That night was a reminder for me of just how much I need a pastor to "[keep] watch over" my soul (Hebrews 13:17). I've written books on relationships, I've spoken on communication, I'm a pastor myself—but I'm often completely blind when it comes to my own sin. And so are you. We need others to overcome sin and grow the way God has planned.

LIVING STONES IN HIS TEMPLE

Another part of the Christian life that flourishes in community is worship. Again, this is something we can also enjoy by ourselves. We can worship anytime, anywhere, and in complete solitude. But something unique and irreplaceable happens when we worship together.

The New Testament captures this double truth when it pictures both individual believers and the family of believers as His temple. You and I are a temple of the Holy Spirit (1 Corinthians 6:19). Yet in the same letter, Paul describes churches as being part of "God's building" (3:9). And when we come together to worship corporately, we respond to God—and He reveals Himself to us—in different ways.

Donald Whitney explains:

God will manifest His presence in congregational worship in ways you can never know even in the most glorious secret worship. That's because you are not only a temple of God as an individual, but the Bible also says (and far more often) that Christians *collectively* are God's temple.... God manifests His presence in different ways to the "living stones" of His temple when they are gathered than He does to them when they are apart (see also Ephesians 2:19–22; 1 Peter 2:5a).

This is why gathering to worship with other believers in a local church is so irreplaceable. It can't be substituted with a great personal devotional time, a lively Bible study with friends, a meditative nature hike, or a live TV church service. When the church is together to worship and to hear God's Word preached, nourishment and encouragement occur that can't happen quite the same anywhere else. Our corporate worship edifies and strengthens us and glorifies God in ways nothing else can.

I hope you're seeing that the things we do together as Christians aren't extracurricular activities. They're not optional benefits to be claimed when we find the time. When we worship, pursue godliness, and live God's Word *together*, we are expressing an integral part of what it means to be His followers.

But if you still think that committing to a local church might be good for other Christians but not for you, consider a very provocative statement...

THE REAL MEANING
OF MEMBERSHIP

My friend Mark Dever has studied and thought a lot about the church. He's the pastor of Capitol Hill Baptist Church in Washington DC and the author of *9 Marks of a Healthy Church*. He also knows how to get people's attention. Mark told me recently that when he speaks on college campuses about the local church, he often begins his talk with this provocative sentence:

> "If you are not a member of the church you regularly attend, you may well be going to hell."

That usually quiets the room.

"I don't mean for a second," Mark goes on to explain, "that you literally have to have your name on a membership card in a church somewhere to go to heaven. I believe in justification by faith alone in Christ alone by God's grace alone. At the same time, in the New Testament it seems that the local church is there to verify or falsify our claims to be Christians. The man in 1 Corinthians 5 who was sleeping with his father's wife thought of himself as a Christian."

Mark's point is that many people in the world claim to be Christians but aren't living a new life. They don't understand or haven't been changed by the gospel. A university student from London bemoaned the choir director at his church who was openly having an affair with the lead soprano. A pastor was distraught over how to handle a member of his worship team who also owned a pornographic bookstore. These are examples of people who need to have the gospel clarified for them. They need to be told that they can't claim to have saving faith and continue to walk in darkness (see 1 John 1:5–10).

Our assurance of salvation must include a changed life. Confidence that we've truly been saved shouldn't rest on an emotional experience or a prayer we prayed during an altar call years ago. "I don't care how much you cry during singing or preaching," Mark Dever states. "If you do not live a life marked by love toward others, the Bible has no encouragement for you to think that you're a Christian. None."

In 1 Peter 2 we're told to make our calling and election sure. How do you do this? One of the most practical steps we can take is to join a local church. The fact is that *you* might be someone who needs to have the gospel and its implications clarified in your life. That's why you need the faithful teaching of God's Word by pastors. You need the protection and godly provocation of having other Christians who are willing to challenge sin in your life.

And you need other Christians whom you can love. The book of 1 John was written to help people identify the evidence of true salvation in their lives. Do you know one of the primary signs we're told to look for? Genuine love for others (see 1 John 2:9–10).

"Do you want to know that your new life is real?" asks Mark Dever. "Commit yourself to a local group of saved sinners. Try to love them. Don't just do it for three weeks. Don't just do it for six months. Do it for years. And I think you'll find out, and others will, too, whether or not you love God. The truth will show itself."

The local church is the place where our new life in Christ is lived out and proven. "Joining a church won't save you," Dever states emphatically. "It's only the death of Christ that saves you. He alone is our righteousness. But if He really is our righteousness, if we really love He who we have not seen, it will show itself by us loving those that we do see."

WHAT HOLDS US BACK

What would loving those we interact with in the family of God look like in your life and mine? What would it mean to be committed to a local church? That's what we'll examine in the next chapter.

But what if you still feel hesitant about taking this step? Maybe you're starting to see that God's plan for the church is beautiful, but you're still distracted by all the things you think are wrong with the churches you've attended.

I won't deny that there are problems. The sad reality is that there are churches and church leaders that grossly misrepresent Jesus Christ through their lives and teaching. And you only need to attend one ineffective, unfriendly, or lethargic church to send all the soaring rhetoric about the bride of Christ falling to earth like a deflated balloon.

But are these experiences really what hold us back from loving the local church? I've come to believe that our generation's biggest obstacles aren't problems in the church, but problems in *us*. We have absorbed attitudes and assumptions from the world around us that have negatively affected what we expect from church and how we approach our role in it.

For example:

- We've adopted self-centered attitudes. We've believed the lie that we'll be happier the less we sacrifice or give of ourselves and our time. But the more we clutch our time, money, and comfort and selfishly refuse to give to our church, the less we receive back.

- We've let proud independence keep us uninvolved. This can be pride that says, "I don't need other people in my life." Or it may be pride that says, "I don't want other people to see me for who I really am." Both forms cut us off from the blessings and benefits of community in the local church.

- We've adopted a critical eye toward the church. We've believed that by complaining or logging our church's faults, we are accomplishing something. But God calls us to repent of our critical spirit and pick up one of concern instead. Genuine concern is what happens when we see a problem and we care. That kind of concern leads to positive changes for us and our church.

Recently my friend David from New York told me how he'd been going to church as a "consumer," focused on comparing and critiquing. He realized he needed to become a "communer" who goes to meet God and express His love to others. God has helped him change from a person who left church each week with a list of complaints to an active servant. "The beautiful part of all this," David said, "is that I'm a lot happier as a communer than I was as a consumer."

Only when you and I reject self-centeredness, prideful independence, and a critical spirit can the beauty of the local church come into focus. Then we'll see that committing to a church isn't a burden, but a gift and a necessity. It doesn't tie us down; it anchors us in the storm of life. And even its faults become an opportunity for us to love and serve.

THE OPEN ROAD

I came across a book by a young Christian author who shared his story of finding God on the open road. He and a buddy packed up for a road trip and hit the highway in search of God. His pastor at home just didn't seem to understand his longings for spiritual depth, so he left everything familiar behind and headed out for adventure.

It made for an interesting book. There's definitely something appealing about striking out and discovering God. It sounds spiritual and courageous. But I don't think it's what God's Word prescribes for spiritual growth. And ultimately I don't think it's as spiritual or as courageous as it might appear.

Going away is easy. Do you want to know what's harder? Do you want to know what takes more courage and what will make you grow faster than anything else? Join a local church and lay down your selfish desires by considering others more important than yourself. Humble yourself and acknowledge that you need other Christians. Invite them into your life. Stop complaining about what's wrong with the church, and become part of a solution.

It's so simple and yet so life-changing. Life lived in a local church is an adventure that will lead to more joy and more spiritual depth than you can imagine. It might not make a bestselling memoir...but it's the story God loves to read.

Chapter 4

JOIN THE CLUB

What Passion in Action Looks Like

Robert lives in Gilbert, Arizona. He likes friends to call him "Fat Bob." He loves life and people and enjoys laughing at himself. He's got a good job and faithfully attends his church. But if you really want to see Robert excited, ask him about his Jeep. He talks about it like it's a person. "She's my baby," he says affectionately. He searched for over two years to find just the right yellow and black Wrangler. "It was spotless. Just gorgeous," he recounts.

"Once I got the Jeep…well, of course I had to join the Jeep club," explains Robert. The local club had over fifteen hundred active members. It offered meetings, parties, trail runs, and a website where members could exchange Jeep tips. "It's a whole Jeep community," Robert says.

Through the club, Robert hooked up with guys who taught him the finer points of four-wheeling. As his Jeep-discipleship intensified, Robert's commitment only deepened. "I was totally hooked," he says. "Every free moment was consumed. I was either working on a Jeep, planning a Jeep run, hanging out and talking Jeep, or going on-line to check our Jeep website."

UNHOOKED

I met Robert at a Christian conference. He came with a group from his church to hear me speak. On the final night I gave a message about the importance of the local church. I started by asking, "Are you married to the church? Or are you dating the church?"

The question unsettled Robert. "God started speaking," he remembers. "He was asking me, 'Robert, what are *you* married to?' And the only thing I could think of was the Jeep club. It was obvious, but I'd never seen it before: I was married to the Jeep club, and I was dating the church!"

In my message I quoted John Stott, who said, "If the church is central to God's purpose as seen in both history and the gospel, it must surely also be central to our lives. How can we take lightly what God takes so seriously?

How dare we push to the circumference what God has placed at the center?"

As his mind played back over the last two years, Robert realized that he had pushed the church to the outskirts of his life. He had invested so much in the Jeep club but very little in his local church. If a Jeep run was scheduled on a Sunday afternoon, he'd be watching the clock throughout the church service, ready to rush out as soon as the sermon was done.

And then there was the Saturday he was asked to help clean up the church property for a special conference that was being held at the building. "I totally blew it off," Robert recalls. "I didn't even give it a second thought. I had promised the guys in the club that I'd help them pick up trash on a trail to prepare for a run.

"The reality is, I had no passion for the church or the people in it," Robert told me. "I would do anything for the guys in the club. But I really struggled if I was asked to give time on the weekend to serve my church."

WHAT'S YOUR CLUB?

What does passion for the church look like in a life? It's not hard to figure out. You and I already have the answer. We already know *exactly* what being passionate about something involves, because we all have our own version of the Jeep club—some interest or pursuit that we care deeply about. It might be a hobby or a sport, a career or an education. It might be a preoccupation with technology, your health, a political party, a cause, or a relationship.

Sometimes the signs of passionate commitment are all there, but we just haven't seen them yet.

I remember sitting next to a man on an airplane who was intently reading a magazine all about model trains. I was baffled that he could find anything interesting in a lengthy article describing the pros and cons of the latest toy train tracks. *Get a life, buddy!* I thought to myself.

Then it hit me. I subscribed to not one, but *two* magazines about Apple computers. I had spent hours reading articles and reviews about iPods, Macintosh laptops, and the latest software. *Maybe I need to get a life,* I concluded.

Take a minute to identify your "club." When you do, there's a good chance you'll see a pattern of what passion looks like in your life. Your passion is what you talk about, think about, and dream about. It's what you give your time to without complaint. It's what you find your identity in. It's what you're willing to sacrifice for.

A PROFILE OF COMMITMENT

Not surprisingly, the New Testament gives us a clear and helpful teaching on what passionate involvement in a local church should look like. Let's look at what you and I need to do to make commitment to Christ the profile of our lives:

1. You join.

Just like Robert and his Jeep Club, when we're passionate, we want to sign up. We want to belong, to be identified as a member. In the same way, it's not enough to just go to church or sample from several churches in your area. You need to officially join—become a member—so that the pastors and others there know you're part of the team.

Hebrews 13:17 urges Christians to obey their leaders, thereby receiving the spiritual benefits that come from having pastors who watch over our souls. But you can't do this well if you haven't joined a church. Becoming a church member gives you specific accountability, care, encouragement, and leadership.

Once you've joined, put down your roots. A common attitude toward the church is, "I'm here...tentatively...at least for the immediate future...I think." But this keeps people from really experiencing church. It's so much better for you and your church when you declare, "I'm here, all of me, and I trust God with my future."

Christian martyr Jim Elliott once said, "Wherever you are, be all there. Live to the hilt every situation you believe to be the will of God." Adopt this mind-set with your local church. Be *all there* with your heart.

2. You make the local church a priority.

We build our lives around our priorities. Building your life around the church means making it the kind of priority that secondary concerns flow *around,* not over. Unfortunately for some, concerns like the Sunday football game, hunting season, skiing, sleeping in, or enjoying beautiful weather are concerns that run *over* their involvement in the church.

Now it might be easy to see that church should come before football. But what about an issue like your job or where you live? Should finding the perfect job, or living in a better city or town, be more important to you than the local church? People relocate all the time for a different climate or a better paying job without considering their church involvement. They assume, "Of course I'll find a good church once I get there." But this isn't always as easy as it sounds.

If God has blessed you with relationships, accountability, and community in the church where you are, I encourage you to give something as significant as a move much prayerful consideration.

The same goes for high school or college students who are choosing a college. Factor in the importance of church to you as you make your decision. I know this is probably a new idea (the local church is *not* a factor listed in the *U.S. News & World Report*'s annual ranking of top schools!). But if you're living for eternity and godliness matters to you, shouldn't church be a top priority?

I'm not saying it's wrong to go away to school. But I think too many students assume they should go away without considering the spiritual implications. My advice is don't go *away to* college or university and *away from* a thriving church experience. I know students from my church who have carefully chosen an out-of-state school where they know there's a strong local church. Then they've been purposeful in getting involved there. Many others have chosen to attend schools nearby so they could stay in our church. Both can be good options if the local church remains a priority.

Ricky, who lives in El Paso, wrestled with this issue. Deciding to attend a school close to home so he could stay in the local church his dad pastors was not easy. "I was getting stacks of mail daily from colleges all over the country, even schools like Cornell and Harvard," he says. "But I saw that where I decided to go to college would be a picture of the rest of my life. Would my career or my family in Christ be my first priority? When you realize that you're only going to be on the earth for a short time, it makes you really want to build something with your life, something that will last," Ricky says. "For me, choosing the right school followed choosing the right church."

3. You try to make your pastor's job a joy.

An important part of commitment involves supporting your pastors. Christians often pray for good leaders, but we should also ask God to help us be good followers. Did you know that God tells us to keep our own self-interest in mind by being the kind of followers that are a joy to lead? Hebrews 13:17 says:

> Obey your leaders and submit to them, for they are keeping watch over your souls, as those who will have to give an account. Let them do this with joy and not with groaning, for that would be of no advantage to you.

This passage reminds us that pastors will give an account to God for how they cared for the people in their churches. It's a reminder that no one will get away with heavy-handed authoritarianism or false teaching that leads people astray. But it also calls us to submit to leaders who are seeking to mature us in the faith. In fact, it tells us to be the type of church members that make our pastors' jobs enjoyable.

How can you do this? First, embrace, obey, and love God's Word personally. Nothing makes a pastor happier than to see a member of his church growing in godliness.

And take it upon yourself to protect your pastor by praying for him and by refusing to engage in slander against him. Leadership isn't easy. It's certainly easier to comment on and critique the job someone else is doing than it is to lead. So don't critique your pastor; pray for him and find ways to encourage him. And if others engage in gossip or slander, challenge them and refuse to participate. When you make your pastor's duties a joy, *you* will benefit spiritually.

4. You find ways to serve.

Serving is spending yourself—energy, time, and gifts— for something outside of yourself. First Peter 4:10 says, "Each one should use whatever gift he has received to serve others, faithfully administering God's grace in its various forms" (NIV).

Serving is the fastest way to feel a sense of ownership in your church. It's also the best way to build relationships. Membership in the church must not be spectatorship. No part of a body can merely observe the work of others—it has to contribute. The church "grows and builds itself up in love, as each part does its work" (Ephesians 4:16, NIV).

Recently I visited a church in Georgia and met a member there named Brad. I learned that he volunteered his time with the church's video team. He was very talented. He had written a software package that his church used in their video production. He volunteered several times a month and helped to train others. He gave time, energy, and money to contribute to his church's mission. As I asked him questions, I discovered that he was also the owner of a successful technology company. "I love what I do at work," he told me. "But serving here at the church is my passion."

Brad embodies the attitude I believe God wants every Christian to have. We might work in a thousand different fields. We might have a thousand different interests. But no matter what we do for a living—whether we're a plumber, a politician, or a CEO—we're called to bring our whole selves into our church family. Instead of being an afterthought, investing our abilities to honor and glorify God in our church should come first.

It seems to me that we go wrong on this issue when we think of our gifts as something we were born with, or skills we acquired (and therefore own) because we studied or trained hard to get them. The truth is, all our gifts and experiences come to us from the good hand of God. "What do you have that you did not receive?" writes Paul (1 Corinthians 4:7).

A passionate disciple is always asking, "What can I do to serve God and others with what He's so generously given me?" Paul says in Romans 12:4–6 that in the local church our gifts belong to each other.

> Just as each of us has one body with many members, and these members do not all have the same function, so in Christ we who are many form one body, *and each member belongs to all the others*. We have different gifts, according to the grace given us. (NIV)

We shouldn't withhold our gifts at church. We shouldn't even wait to be called on to exercise them. Instead we should humbly present our gifts to our leaders and offer to serve the needs of the whole body in whatever way would be most helpful.

5. You give.

Money is a tangible return for what we have invested of ourselves—in time, abilities, business choices, and other personal resources. So for a Christian, giving financially is a very meaningful expression of worship. It's a way to offer up our lives to Him. When we tithe (giving 10 percent of our income) and contribute money in other ways to our local church, we're telling God that we trust Him and acknowledge that all we have belongs to Him. God challenged the Israelites:

> "Bring the whole tithe into the storehouse, that there may be food in my house. Test me in this," says the LORD Almighty, "and see if I will not throw open the floodgates of heaven and pour out so much blessing that you will not have room enough for it." (Malachi 3:10, NIV)

Many worthy and wonderful ministry opportunities exist all over the world. But because the local church is the place you're nourished spiritually, it should be the first place you invest financially. If you've never taken the step to obey God through faithful giving, let me urge you to begin the adventure today. God will give you new joy as you trust Him with your finances. In Matthew 6:19–20,

Jesus promises that everything we give to Him is converted to treasure and reward in heaven that will never fade! (For more guidance on giving, I recommend *The Treasure Principle,* by my friend Randy Alcorn [Sisters, OR: Multnomah Publishers, 2001].)

6. *You connect with people.*

Passion for the church involves diving into the community of the local church. It means "doing life" with other Christians by pursuing relationships that extend beyond the church building and official church functions.

The New Testament word for this experience is *fellowship*. We've grown so accustomed to the word that it has lost its meaning and power. Fellowship isn't just two or more people in the same room. "Fellowship is a uniquely Christian relational experience," writes my friend and fellow pastor John Loftness. "Fellowship is participating together in the life and truth made possible by the Holy Spirit through our union with Christ. Fellowship is sharing something in common at the deepest possible level of human relationships—our experience of God himself."

Fellowship means belonging to each other. The New Testament is full of instruction on what it means for us to belong to each other. Have you ever noticed the "one another" commands in Scripture? Here's a sampling of what we're called to do in our relationships with other Christians. We're to:

- Love one another (John 13:34).
- Be devoted to one another (Romans 12:5).
- Honor one another (Romans 12:10).
- Rejoice with one another (Romans 12:15).
- Serve one another (Galatians 5:13).
- Carry one another's burdens (Galatians 6:2).
- Forgive one another (Ephesians 4:32).
- Encourage one another (1 Thessalonians 5:11).
- Offer hospitality to one another (1 Peter 4:9).
- Confess our sins to one another (James 5:16).
- Pray for one another (James 5:16).

Every "one another" command shows that the church isn't merely about programs or meetings, but about *shared life*. Your church might have small group environments that facilitate friendships. But even if it doesn't, you can pursue them. So start reaching out to others. Offer hospitality. Find practical ways to serve others. Don't wait for someone else to make the first move. Take the initiative and invite them into your life.

The opportunity to share life with other Christians and experience this kind of fellowship is one of the most exciting parts of being a committed member of a local church. But it requires effort and hard work. We have to pursue it diligently.

As you reach out to others don't limit yourself to people just like you. The beauty of the local church is the opportunity you have to grow close to people from completely different backgrounds and cultures. So if you're single, develop friendships with married couples and families. If you're older, look for the chance to befriend younger members. Don't let age, race, or any other factor distance you from other brothers and sisters in Christ.

7. You share your passion.

Have you ever noticed that people who have been captured by an idea or a product almost instinctively try to get other people excited about it, too? In the same way, when you're transformed by the gospel and you're passionate about the church, you want others to experience your joy. Passion spills out. You can't keep it inside.

Passionate involvement in a local church should never be viewed as a way to escape the world. As I've said, the local church is God's primary means to reach the world. That's why an important part of church is expressing a heart for the lost. Look for ways that you can creatively, naturally, enthusiastically reach those who don't yet know Christ personally.

YOU CAN THRIVE

As you'd expect, the ways you express commitment in a local church are also the essential elements of thriving there. This is true even for new Christians.

My wife, Shannon, was saved a year after graduating from college. Everything about Christianity was brand-new. She hadn't grown up singing "Father Abraham" as a kid or watching Bible stories acted out on felt boards. She didn't know Jonah from Adam! She was like a tender seedling just pushing out of the ground—in need of nourishment, with no elaborate system of roots from which to draw sustenance.

I met Shannon three years after God saved her. The young woman I fell in love with had a passion for her Savior, a humility and an understanding of grace that belied the short time she'd been a Christian. The spiritual seedling had grown rapidly into a thriving young sapling.

What made it possible for Shannon to flourish in her faith in such a brief period of time? Ultimately it was the grace of God in her life. But I believe a key conduit of this grace was her purposeful involvement in the local church.

Shannon rooted herself in the local church—even when it seemed costly. She set aside plans to move to Nashville to pursue a career in music so that she could stay and mature in the community of believers she had come to love. Shannon threw herself into the life of the church. She didn't just attend on Sundays—she grabbed every opportunity to be with and learn from strong Christians. She participated in a small group and formed close friendships there. She moved from her dad's house forty minutes away to the basement apartment of a family in the church who lived much closer. She babysat for them and other families. She went on a mission trip. And every Friday she sang on the college worship team.

Shannon's journals from those early days are full of notes from Sunday sermons, reflections on her personal Bible study, prayer requests from girlfriends in her small group, and her own written petitions to God. What is evident on every page is that God's family was her new passion. And she demonstrated that passion with action.

GETTING A REAL LIFE

Remember Robert and his Jeep? After being challenged at the conference to stop dating the church, he resolved to change his life. The day he got home he logged onto the Jeep website and posted his final message to the club. "I explained that I was no longer going to be a member," Robert said happily. "I announced that I was divorcing the Jeep club and marrying the church!"

These days Robert still loves to talk Jeep. But if you want to see him really excited, ask him about his church. There's passion in his voice when he talks about it. "The church isn't just an option for me," he says. "It's a lifeline. It's something I really want. I look forward to it…like I did with the trail runs. I'm excited to go to church and to serve. And I'm happy to say that I am still married to the church," Robert says proudly. "In fact, I just celebrated my first anniversary."

Chapter 5

CHOOSING YOUR CHURCH

The Ten Things That Matter Most

The first time Curtis saw the congregation at our church he wasn't too excited. "As a black man, I had always enjoyed the comforts of segregated churches," Curtis told me later. "When I walked in here, all these folks were singing and had their hands raised to God." Curtis paused and a playful smile spread across his face. "Man, there were so many white hands in the air, I thought it was snowing!"

In spite of his misgivings, Curtis stayed for the meeting. He even came back the next Sunday. He was drawn to the teaching and the depth of faith he saw in other singles at the church. He decided to stay and become a part of this fellowship.

Not that the choice was easy for him. "It had never crossed my mind to go to a church that was predominantly white," he says. "When you're black in this country, with all of the history of racism, apart from the saving knowledge of Jesus, your blackness is sometimes all you have left. It totally defines you. But God showed me that I was a Christian first and a black man second. The gospel had to define me. Being in a place that preached and lived the gospel had to be the priority."

WHAT MATTERS MOST

If you're ready to decide where to go to church—or not sure if the church you're attending is where God wants you—you may be faced with difficult choices as well. A lot is at stake. Most of us have a lot of options. And most of us have a lot of preferences, too.

So how do we decide what matters most?

The wisdom you need to choose a church is a little like the wisdom a person needs to choose a spouse. For example, it's not wrong for a woman to want to marry a man with blond hair who likes Italian food and hiking. But it would be foolish to place these preferences over the priority of his being truly converted and growing in godliness. In the same way, it's not wrong to want a church with a lot of people your age or to prefer a certain style of worship music—but these are secondary concerns. Curtis's example is helpful. He chose a church based on the criteria God's Word gives—not just on his preferences, or what felt comfortable or familiar to him.

In the same way, we need two different lists when it comes to selecting a church—a "must-have" list and a "that-would-be-nice" list of qualities in a church.

In this chapter, I want to help you with your "must-have" list.

TEN IMPORTANT QUESTIONS

Use these ten questions to help you explore and understand a church you're considering. They work whether you've been there for two weeks or ten years. This list isn't exhaustive, and some of the questions will take time to process. But they can help you hone in on the issues that matter most.

1. Is this a church where God's Word is faithfully taught?

"The kind of church you want to be a part of," writes Donald Whitney, "is one where, when the Bible is read at the beginning of a sermon, you can be confident that what follows will be built upon it. God made our hearts, and only He knows what we need most. And He made our hearts for the Word of God. Nothing nourishes us like His message."

A God-glorifying church is governed by God's Word. Paul tells us in 2 Timothy 3:16 that "all Scripture is breathed out by God and profitable for teaching, for reproof, for correction, and for training in righteousness."

Be careful here. At first glance, most churches will appear to teach God's Word. You'll see it printed in the bulletin, written on the walls, or sprinkled through the services. But these references to Scripture don't necessarily mean a church is submitted to God's Word.

Some teachers start their messages with the Bible, but it's only a jumping-off point to share their own opinions. I should know—I used to be one of those teachers! I used to build entertaining messages around engaging illustrations, stories, or ideas I had. I always peppered my messages with Scripture. But Scripture wasn't the meat of the message; it was only the seasoning.

Since then, God has mercifully helped me to grow in my understanding of faithful preaching. I've learned that the best thing I can do for my church is to build a message on the teaching of a particular passage of Scripture—to draw my points and emphasis from the points and emphasis of the passage. This approach, often called expositional preaching, can be expressed through many different personalities and presentation styles (and it doesn't have to add up to long, difficult, or boring sermons!). The driving principle is that God's Word has the authority. The preacher's task is simply to unleash what it has to say to God's people.

So your first priority is to look for a church whose teaching is driven by a confidence in the authority of Scripture.

2. Is this a church where sound doctrine matters?

Acts 2:42 says that the first believers "devoted themselves to the apostles' teaching." Today we have the apostles' teaching passed down in the Bible. *Doctrine* may sound like an intimidating word. But it simply means what the Bible teaches about any given subject. Therefore, a church in which doctrine matters is one that values biblical truth, knows what it believes, and is guided by these beliefs in the way it functions.

Sound doctrine is always under attack. Paul tells us in 2 Timothy 4:3–4 that "the time is coming when people will not endure sound teaching, but having itching ears they will accumulate for themselves teachers to suit their own passions, and will turn away from listening to the truth and wander off into myths."

These days, doctrine is often derided by people who view it as divisive and unnecessary to living the Christian life. Some people pride themselves on not being concerned with the specifics of what they believe about salvation, sin, the work of the Spirit, and other doctrinal issues. A friend who attended a large conference for youth workers told me that the host started the event by walking onstage and declaring, "It's not about doctrine! It's about Jesus!"

I consider this a sad and misleading statement. We don't have to choose between caring about doctrine and loving Jesus. The two pursuits are not opposed to each other. In fact, they are inseparable! We can only grow in our love for our Savior as we learn more of who He is and what He has accomplished for us. A concern for truth doesn't take us away from a deeper relationship with Him. It leads us closer to Him, in greater worship, adoration, and obedience.

I agree that you can find churches that hold to their doctrinal positions arrogantly or unwisely. Or that use secondary doctrinal issues as a way to be exclusive or condescending toward others who disagree with them. I hope you'll never fall into this kind of attitude. We can love truth deeply without being unkind or proud.

Look for a church that clearly knows and defines what it believes—a place where the statement of faith actually makes a difference. If this is the church home for you, you should be able to agree with this statement on its major doctrines.

If you're looking for a book that can add insight to your Bible study on doctrine, I highly recommend *Bible Doctrine* by Wayne Grudem. This book covers all the major doctrines—of God, man, Christ, salvation—in a way that's easy to understand. Shannon, who often uses it in her devotions, has found that Grudem's teaching infuses her heart with love for her Father in heaven. A helpful teaching tool like this can also clarify your own doctrinal convictions as you look for a church home.

3. Is this a church in which the gospel is cherished and clearly proclaimed?

The gospel is the Good News of Jesus Christ's perfect life, sacrificial death for sinners, and glorious resurrection and ascension. It's the story line of all of God's Word—a holy God has mercifully made a way for sinners to be forgiven and accepted through the cross of Christ.

I grew up in a Christian home, but for many years of my life the gospel wasn't a central focus. In fact it was all rather fuzzy. I knew Jesus loved me. I knew He wanted a personal relationship with me. I knew He wanted me to be a good person.

It wasn't until God brought me to a church that clearly proclaimed and cherished the gospel that I learned how the work of Christ for me functioned practically in my daily Christian life. I could only relate to God on the basis of His grace. My good works didn't earn my standing before God; Jesus had earned my standing before Him. I wasn't just a lovable guy in need of a personal relationship; I was a sinner who needed to be rescued from God's just wrath by the death of Jesus. Focusing on this sweet truth made grace truly amazing. It helped me when I was struggling against sin. It helped me to readily forgive others.

About choosing a church, Charles Spurgeon once said:

> Do not go where it is all fine music and grand talk
> and beautiful architecture; those things will neither
> fill anybody's stomach, nor feed his soul. Go where
> the gospel is preached, the gospel that really feeds
> your soul, and go often.

C. J. Mahaney, the pastor and friend who has coached and trained me in ministry, has taught me the primacy of the gospel in my personal life and in leading a local church. He has taught me that the gospel isn't just for getting saved—it's the defining reality we need to live in every day of our lives. That's why I highly recommend his book *The Cross Centered Life* to help you understand what it means to cherish and live in the good of the gospel.

And for help in understanding how a focus on the Cross shapes a church's approach to ministry, I recommend D. A. Carson's outstanding book *The Cross and Christian Ministry*.

4. Is this a church committed to reaching non-Christians with the gospel?

Jesus commissioned every follower to go and make disciples (see Matthew 28:18–20). So make it a priority to look for a church that not only celebrates the gospel, but also reaches out to the unsaved in the community with this same Good News.

Without an emphasis on evangelism, a church becomes selfish and ingrown. Some churches can become so preoccupied with being relevant to the surrounding culture that they lose all distinctiveness. But the clear message of the gospel should never be altered to make it more marketable. People separated from God by their sin are never served when a church places relevance above its mission of faithfully proclaiming the gospel.

5. Is this a church whose leaders are characterized by humility and integrity?

On my twenty-first birthday, my dad wrote me a special letter in which he encouraged me to find men I wanted to be like. "Then sit at their feet and learn from them," he wrote. It's good advice. No pastor is perfect, but when it comes to evaluating a church's leaders, you want to find men you can trust and whose example you can follow.

First Timothy 3 lists the qualifications for pastors: A leader in the church must be a man who is above reproach, sober-minded, self-controlled, respectable, hospitable, not violent but gentle, not quarrelsome, not a lover of money. Notice that the qualifications relate mostly to the quality of his life. It's been said that pastoring is a character profession. No amount of skill, leadership ability, or communication skills can replace godly character. Look for a church where personal character is of higher importance than title, position, or outward success.

I've found that the most effective leaders view themselves first as servants. And leaders with integrity keep themselves accountable. They don't view themselves as being immune to sin, but build safeguards around themselves financially, morally, and in every other category to keep themselves from compromise. They see themselves as servants of the Great Shepherd—and live in light of their accountability to Him.

6. Is this a church where people strive to live by God's Word?

No church can claim to live out God's Word perfectly. What's important is to look for a church that is seeking not only to believe rightly, but also to *live* rightly. It's possible for a church to be doctrinally sound but have a culture of total apathy when it comes to applying the truth of God's Word in everyday life.

Our faith in God and our desire to honor Him with obedience and holiness will affect everything—from how we conduct ourselves at work to how we speak to our children at home. If it doesn't, something is wrong.

That means that the church you're looking for will seek to build a culture and community of both hearing and obeying God's Word (see James 1:22). It will seek not only to win converts, but to make disciples by helping them to mature in godly living in every area of life.

7. Is this a church where I can find and cultivate godly relationships?

We all need relationships where we can receive encouragement, accountability, and care. And an essential part of living out God's Word is being connected to other Christians.

Does the church you're considering provide settings where you can enjoy biblical fellowship, mutual encouragement, and application of Scripture? This will look different at different churches—some have official small-group structures; others don't, but achieve the same purpose through other means. What matters is that godly relationships happen. And of course, these kinds of relationships usually take time to develop.

Finally, think about whether you'll be able to invest adequately in the relationship opportunities the church offers. No matter how great the church, if you live two hours away you'll be very limited in your ability to be a meaningful part of the community. The local church you choose should indeed be *local*.

8. Is this a church where members are challenged to serve?

Pastors are not supposed to be paid professionals who do ministry in place of their members. Ephesians 4:12 tells us that pastors are to *"equip the saints for the work of ministry, for building up the body of Christ."* That means you should look for a church that equips its members to serve and minister, and then challenges them to do so.

I want to caution you about how you apply this criterion. I've met people who evaluate opportunities to serve in a very self-centered way. For example, they're motivated to serve, but only in their preferred way. If you don't make this opportunity available, they leave in a huff. When you think about it, that attitude is funny: True service means giving cheerfully to meet someone else's genuine need—and the most important need probably isn't the server's need to serve in a particular way!

My advice, then, is to make sure you're not evaluating a church primarily by its capacity as a stage to showcase your gifts. Look for a place that will challenge you to care deeply about the needs of others. Then be ready to do whatever it takes to meet those needs.

9. Is this a church that is willing to kick me out?

This priority might sound old-fashioned to you. But there's a hard, important truth here. When a person who claims to be a Christian lives in a way that blatantly contradicts all that it means to be a disciple of Christ, a faithful church's responsibility is to begin the process of removing that person from membership and to treat him or her like an unbeliever in the hope that he or she will repent and ultimately be restored (see 1 Corinthians 5; 2 Corinthians 2). This is not harsh or abrupt. This practice is called church discipline and was instituted by Jesus (see Matthew 18).

Why should you be excited about the potential of being expelled from a church? I gain a wonderful sense of protection in knowing that if I committed a scandalous sin and showed no repentance, my church wouldn't put up with it. They would plead with me to change. They would patiently confront me with God's Word. And eventually, if I refused to change, they would lovingly kick me out.

Remember that the purpose behind church discipline is first to restore. Four hundred years ago Menno Simons wrote: "We do not want to expel any, but rather to receive; not to amputate, but rather to heal; not to discard, but rather to win back; not to grieve, but rather to comfort; not to condemn, but rather to save." So church discipline is an expression of love. It's a way to try to restore a sinning brother as well as a way to protect the witness of the church.

After all, the power of a church in a community starts with its example. As our generation knows too well, hypocrisy destroys a church's witness and leaves its message discredited. A church committed to glorifying God and reaching the lost world will not only have membership, but will clearly define what that membership requires. It will want to be able to answer clearly anyone who asks who is truly part of the church and who is not.

Discipline is also important when someone begins spreading false teaching. In these cases, discipline guards the church against the damaging effects of heresy.

So look for a church that will not only welcome you into membership, but will lovingly hold you to your commitments as a Christian—a church that will love you enough to put you out of fellowship for the good of your soul.

10. Is this a church I'm willing to join "as is" with enthusiasm and faith in God?

I've often advised men and women not to marry someone if their unspoken plan is to change them "into the person they ought to be." Ask anyone who's been married more than a year. It just doesn't work.

In your church quest, ask yourself, "Can I joyfully and fully support this church's leaders, their teachings, and the direction they have set?"

Please don't join a church because you think God has called you to overhaul it! Humbly recognize that you have your own sin to deal with and that you won't succeed anywhere as a self-appointed leader.

Find a church you can be excited about. Of course, you'll want your church to grow and improve (as you yourself hopefully will!). But if it's the one for you, you should be ready to join it "as is"—that is, join it with faith that God is at work. Leave your gripes and complaints at the door. Those attitudes will only detract from your experience, limit your involvement, and weaken the church's unity.

YOUR ATTITUDE COUNTS

Let me encourage you not only to ask the right questions about the churches you visit, but to ask them with the right attitude. Approach every church you visit with humility. Pray for every church you visit. Ask God to help you see the good in each church. Even if it's not the right church for you, remember how much God loves the work of a church even when it's being carried out imperfectly.

And don't get stuck in church-hopping, church-shopping mode. Do your best to find a good church as quickly as possible. If you're feeling overwhelmed by too many points, boil them all down to three:

- You want a church that *teaches* God's Word.
- You want a church that *values* God's Word.
- You want a church that *lives* God's Word.

These are the nonnegotiables.

You won't find any church that perfectly meets all the qualifications we've discussed (you certainly won't find "perfect" at my church!). But be encouraged. Churches that are committed to growing in the right ways do exist. They are out there. They're not confined to one denomination or worship style. God is at work around the world. And these churches need committed and selfless men and women to join them in their mission for Christ.

TOUGH SITUATIONS

This chapter was difficult for me to write. I don't want anyone—least of all a fellow pastor—to think I'm setting myself up as a judge of other churches. At the same time, the foundational elements that we have explored are scriptural and truly important. If they're completely missing, a church isn't merely imperfect; it's disobedient and dishonoring to God.

The sad fact is that bad churches are out there. These are churches that have abandoned the authority of God's Word or who selectively apply it. These are churches that have neglected the gospel or added to or distorted it.

It grieves me to say it, but there are some churches I would strongly encourage you to leave. I want to say that clearly because the last thing I want is for this book to be used to convince any person to stay in a bad church. We are called to be committed to the church. But sometimes that commitment involves leaving an unbiblical church.

What should you do if you're in a bad church and need to leave?

My encouragement is to make a priority of leaving humbly and as helpfully as possible. Refuse to participate in gossip about members or the leaders in the church. If you're a member, communicate your concerns to the pastor and your points of disagreement. Look for ways to point out examples of grace and to encourage them. Ask to hear their perspective. Your goal should be to leave in a way that is gracious and honoring to God.

What if there aren't any good churches near you?

First, pray that God would strengthen and refine the churches in your area. And don't let your situation excuse you from participation. Find the best church you can, and then throw yourself into learning and serving there. Again, don't set yourself up as the "long-awaited bringer of change." Serve humbly. Serve the leadership. Ask God to use you.

If you're still in a setting where you don't feel you're growing, it may be time for you to move to another area to find the right local church. People pick up and move for a higher paying job without anyone questioning their decision. Why shouldn't we consider moving to place ourselves and our families in a local church where we can reap invaluable, eternal spiritual benefits? I don't encourage this lightly. It's a decision that will take a lot of patience, prayer, counsel, and consideration. But I can speak from personal experience that moving for the right church is something you won't regret. In fact, many people I know who have moved for the right church only regret that they didn't do it sooner.

If it's impossible to move, then trust that God can grow you and use you right where you are. Participate in the best church you can find; then if necessary supplement your spiritual diet with biblical preaching from other sources—on-line or on CD or tape. Read good theological books like the ones I've recommended throughout this chapter.

THE BEST DAYS OF YOUR LIVES

And don't give up. A good church is worth waiting for, praying for, and searching out. God is faithful. He'll provide the right church home for you in His perfect timing.

When God brings you the church family He has for you, cherish what you've been given…and don't let go. Because you've finally found the place where you and your family are going to enjoy the best days of your lives.

That's what the next chapter is about.

Chapter 6

RESCUING SUNDAY

How to Get More from the Best Day of the Week

On Sundays, Christians go to church. Everybody knows that. Church attendance may be slipping around the world, but for a good number of people it's still something we do. It's a habit—like sleeping, breathing…and all the other things we do without thinking.

And I suppose that's the problem. We could do it in our sleep. Some of us do.

I figure I have lived through over fifteen hundred Sunday meetings. On far too many of those Sundays, I have…

- woken up late,
- walked into church groggy,

- worshiped distractedly,
- listened occasionally,
- left early,
- and remembered very little.

But Sundays like that don't deliver much spiritual punch, do they? Looking back, I'm aware of how much I could have gained if more of my Sundays had been prepared for in advance, fully enjoyed, and engaged in with vigor and purpose. Because the truth is, Sunday for a child of God is the best day of the week. For us, those few hours have a strategic and irreplaceable value. They're meant to be packed with promise, full of surprises, pulsing with life.

Why would anyone want to miss out on that?

If you need to rescue Sunday from disrepair, I think this chapter might help you. The best place to start, I've found, is to get rid of what doesn't work. In my case, I found that I needed to lose some harmful attitudes, throw out some bad habits, leave behind some old assumptions (most of which weren't working anyway), and then take practical steps to change the way I go to church.

If you put even a few of my suggestions to work, you'll notice a difference right away. I guarantee it.

We see in Genesis that God takes a day a week for

renewal very seriously. He made Sabbath-keeping one of the Ten Commandments. But if you're worried that I'm going to try to convince you that Sunday is the new Sabbath for Christians, you're wrong. I don't believe that Christians are called to observe the Old Testament laws about Sabbath-keeping.

Still, I think we're missing out on enormous personal and spiritual blessings when we treat Sunday like any other day. Because it isn't. The early church called it "the Lord's day." It's a day to "receive and embrace," as Matthew Henry said, "as a privilege and a benefit, not as a task and a drudgery."

I think you'll discover that God has something for you that will radically change your church experience—because Sundays have come to us as one of His sweetest gifts.

HIS DAY

We first need to see Sunday with new eyes. Of course, in one sense it's just an ordinary day—twenty-four hours during which the sun rises and sets. But when your heart begins to beat for God's glory and God's people and you begin to glimpse His longing to visit *you*, Sunday changes. Actually, it becomes something extraordinary. Something sacred. Something essential.

Every day belongs to God. But Sunday is the Lord's day in a special way. Jesus has owned it uniquely ever since that first Easter when He stepped out of the empty tomb. Think of it. On that morning, for the first time, He had conquered death. He had atoned for our sin. He had made a way for us to come boldly into the presence of the Father. And every Sunday since has been an anniversary of that amazing morning. The Savior has risen—and everything has changed.

This crucified and risen Jesus has promised to be present in a special way when His people gather to worship Him. Wherever Christ's followers gather for church— whether in a cathedral or under a tree—we glorify God, grow in our faith, and encourage each other. And through every minute of it, Jesus is *with* us.

"We must never, therefore," writes J. I. Packer, "let our Sundays become mere routine engagements; in that attitude of mind, we shall trifle them away by a humdrum formality. Every Sunday is meant to be a great day, and we should approach it expectantly, in full awareness of this."

My premise in this chapter is that you and I are very likely to be missing out on God's best for the day unless we learn to *build our week around Sunday,* and not the other way around. For example, we should develop a practical game plan for what happens before, during, and after the Sunday meeting.

Let me show you what I mean.

BEFORE THE MEETING

Do we really need to prepare for Sunday? If we have something to wear and our hair is combed, what's the big deal? But getting ready for Sunday is more than putting on clean clothes and making a quick run past the mirror. We need to get our hearts ready.

It makes sense, really. We shouldn't expect a rich spiritual experience on Sunday if we're not willing to prepare our hearts and minds. Think about other parts of life: Before we play sports, we warm up. Before a big presentation at work, we review our notes. Before we take a major test, we study. Why should we assume that we can show up on Sunday with no spiritual preparation?

Preparing for Sunday involves making both spiritual and practical decisions. On the practical side, a great Sunday starts Saturday night. It begins with carefully deciding what you do and don't do the night before. One of the wisest decisions you can make is to get to bed on time so that you're rested and ready for the next morning.

Besides getting adequate sleep, ask yourself what activities will put you in a God-focused state of mind. What's going to draw you closer to a spirit of prayer and worship? When you stay up late Saturday to watch a movie or surf the Internet, do you wake up refreshed and with God's Word on your lips? Not me. My heart feels dull, and I'm likely to walk into church with some silly action scene playing in my head.

Pastor John Piper believes that turning off the TV can be one of the best ways to prepare your heart to receive God's Word:

> It astonishes me how many Christians watch the same banal, empty, silly, trivial, titillating, suggestive, immodest TV shows that most unbelievers watch—and then wonder why their spiritual lives are weak and their worship experience is shallow with no intensity. If you really want to hear the Word of God the way He means to be heard in truth and joy and power, turn off the television on Saturday night and read something true and great and beautiful and pure and honorable and excellent and worthy of praise (see Philippians 4:8). Then watch your heart un-shrivel and begin to hunger for the Word of God.

God means for His Word to be heard in "truth and joy and power," but that requires a purposeful pursuit of personal holiness. James 1:21 says, "Therefore, get rid of all moral filth and the evil that is so prevalent and humbly accept the word planted in you, which can save you" (NIV).

Prepare your heart.

I encourage you to make your heart ready to receive God's Word not only by avoiding worldly entertainment but by carving out time Saturday night to read God's Word and pray. This will give you a chance to search your heart for any sin against God or others.

It's not too much to ask, really. Consider that you're gathering with God's people to worship the Holy One. Psalm 24:3–5 asks:

> Who may ascend the hill of the LORD?
>> Who may stand in his holy place?
> He who has clean hands and a pure heart,
>> who does not lift up his soul to an idol
>> or swear by what is false.
> He will receive blessing from the LORD
>> and vindication from God his Savior. (NIV)

True, we can only stand before God because Jesus died for our sins in our place. And we can always draw near to God because Jesus is our mediator (1 Timothy 2:5). But instead of making us spiritually lazy, these truths should motivate us humbly to acknowledge any known sin and ask God to forgive us. Reflecting on our need for the gospel is a wonderful preparation for Sunday worship. It helps us to get our minds off our daily preoccupations and prepares our hearts to humbly receive God's Word.

On Sunday morning, wake up early enough to give yourself time to get ready for church and spend some unhurried moments in God's Word and in prayer. Psalm 19 is another wonderful passage to meditate on before the Sunday meeting. It reminds us of the preciousness of God's Word and our need for His help to keep our hearts blameless before Him:

> The ordinances of the LORD are sure
>   and altogether righteous.
> They are more precious than gold,
>   than much pure gold;
> they are sweeter than honey,
>   than honey from the comb.
> By them is your servant warned;
>   in keeping them there is great reward.

Who can discern his errors?
  Forgive my hidden faults.
Keep your servant also from willful sins;
  may they not rule over me.
Then will I be blameless,
  innocent of great transgression.
May the words of my mouth and
    the meditation of my heart
  be pleasing in your sight,
O LORD, my Rock and my Redeemer. (vv. 9–14,
NIV)

Take time, then, to thank God for His Word and for His goodness in saving you. Recount His many blessings in your life.

You may also need to take a hard look at other intrusions on your Sunday experience. I have to confess I'm a news junkie. But on Sunday mornings, the newspaper, news websites, or listening to National Public Radio in my car can be huge distractions, so I avoid them. Worrying about the latest news from abroad just doesn't prepare me to come before a holy and transcendent God.

What are your Sunday morning distractions? Maybe it's work around the house or video games. Maybe it's unrealistic expectations for what your family can actually accomplish before you have to leave for church. Whatever it is, face it and deal with it. Do whatever it takes to protect the "great day" ahead and help your family and friends arrive at church with ready, expectant hearts.

DURING THE MEETING

When you walk into church, remember the eternal significance of what you're joining. You are gathering with the people of God. You've come to worship God, and He will be present by His Holy Spirit.

As the meeting starts, remember that you're not here to be entertained. You're not part of an audience—you're part of a congregation. You stand before the Audience of One. What matters isn't whether you have a good voice, or whether you like the song or the style of music being played. What matters isn't even what you feel.

Worshiping with song is a chance to sing truth and express praise and gratefulness to God. So don't live by your feelings in this moment. Instead, focus your mind on the truth of what you sing and the Person to whom you're singing. God is observing and receiving your worship. In light of the wonderful, gracious God He is, give it your all.

Be careful how you hear.

The sermon is the most important part of the Sunday meeting. And believe me, I'm not saying that because I'm a preacher who's looking for a little appreciation. The importance of the sermon has nothing to do with the stature of the pastor who is preaching and everything to do with the authority and power of the Word of God.

When God's Word is preached to us, in a very real sense God is speaking. As my fellow pastor Jeff Purswell puts it, "When God's Word is being preached, you're not merely receiving information about God. God Himself is *addressing* you through His Word."

And this is why the way we listen to preaching is so important. We shouldn't be passive observers. How we listen and apply what we hear either honors or dishonors God. "Congregations never honor God more than by reverently listening to His Word with a full purpose of praising and obeying Him once they see what He has done and is doing, and what they are called to do," writes J. I. Packer.

I wonder if you've ever considered this: *Listening to preaching is a form of worship.* Donald Whitney explains:

> We normally think of worship as something *we* do, and since preaching is done by the preacher

[and not us], many fail to think of preaching as worship. But *listening* to preaching *is* something you do, and it is an act of worship when you listen with an eager mind and responsive heart. The reason it is an act of *worship* is that you are listening to *God* speak [through His Word].

Because God is speaking, we need to realize our responsibility as we listen. Hearing the truth obligates us to respond to it. Jesus told us, "Therefore consider carefully how you listen" (Luke 8:18, NIV).

To be honest, it took me a while to come around to this way of thinking. In fact, I tended to assume that if a preacher wasn't funny or didn't tell good stories, then I was under no obligation to be fully engaged. This assumption is both convenient and wrong. The real burden of responsibility on Sunday morning is not on the preacher to perform, but on the *congregation* to listen. Don't misunderstand, I'm not justifying or encouraging sloppy or boring sermons. Pastors should strive to make their sermons easy to understand and to engage the attention of their listeners. But ultimately, it's still the responsibility of the people hearing a sermon to listen carefully and apply the truth they hear.

As my pastor C. J. Mahaney has taught me, I will be

held accountable for what I have heard regardless of whether it moved me emotionally. (If you're brave, I encourage you to read that sentence again.) God's truth is God's truth. It doesn't matter if it was delivered with pizzazz or introduced with a tearjerker illustration. If I have heard God's truth, then I am called to obey it. Period.

I encourage you to express your commitment to listen carefully by bringing your Bible and whatever will allow you to record key points from a sermon. Note-taking can take many forms. Don't think that you need to be a stenographer who records everything word for word. Think of your notes as memory joggers to help you leave church with the big ideas firmly in mind.

After the Meeting

As the Sunday meeting comes to a close you'll be given a chance to express your worship to God through the way you love and encourage those around you. John Piper encourages his church to come "on the lookout for God and leave on the lookout for people."

Our faith and love for God is always expressed in our love for others. So try to find people who are new in your church or who don't appear to know others. A new Christian named Lynn dropped me a note: "I don't think people who have grown up going to church know how hard it is to walk into a new setting and feel comfortable," she said. She had visited several churches but left feeling lonely every time because no one took the time to greet her or get to know her.

My family loves to use Sundays whenever we can to invite people to our home. It's the perfect day for fellowship with others and a time when you can reflect together on what God spoke through the message.

How should you spend the rest of your Sunday? I think that there's good reason to reclaim our whole Sunday for pursuing God. This doesn't mean we adopt harsh standards of what we can and can't do, but that each of us considers how we can maximize the potential of Sunday for our spiritual refreshment.

Recently, my wife and I read our daughter some of the Little House books about Laura Ingalls Wilder's childhood during the late 1800s. Laura recounts the experience of her father, whose parents strictly enforced "rest" on the Sabbath. Unfortunately for his family, this meant no play, fun, or enjoyment of any kind. They had to sit in their uncomfortable Sunday clothes and read Bible stories all day. For Laura's father, Sunday during his childhood was no doubt the *worst* day of the week.

What a sad application of honoring the Lord's Day!

Sunday should be a day we enjoy to the fullest for God's glory. It's a chance to take a breather from all the hectic pursuits of the week and reinvigorate ourselves spiritually. It's a way to prepare our hearts for all the challenges and temptations we'll face as the rest of the week unfolds.

So I don't have rules for you as much as possibilities. What would be possible in your family, for example, if you asked yourself this question:

> "How could my family and I invest joyfully in all of Sunday in a way that truly celebrates God's love and presence in our lives—and helps us carry this celebration over into the rest of our week?"

The Puritans called the Lord's Day the "market day for the soul." By that they meant that Sunday was a day for stocking up spiritually for the week ahead. Ask what you could do to "stock up" more successfully. Because no matter how you spend Sunday, Monday always shows up before you know it.

Do what it says.

For a lot of us the weekly schedule of school, work, and the hectic pace of life seems to all but erase what we experienced at church. But this doesn't have to be the case.

Sunday should not only be something we look forward to and anticipate, but also something we draw from as the week unfolds. To get the most benefit from Sunday's worship and message, I encourage you to seek to review and apply what you learned throughout your week. James 1:22–25 says:

> Do not merely listen to the word, and so deceive yourselves. Do what it says. Anyone who listens to the word but does not do what it says is like a man who looks at his face in a mirror and, after looking at himself, goes away and immediately forgets what he looks like. But the man who looks intently into the perfect law that gives freedom, and continues to do this, not forgetting what he has heard, but doing it—he will be blessed in what he does. (NIV)

Don't think that listening is enough. That's a deception, as James tells us. Hearing truth doesn't change us. We have to take action. A member of my church named Dave shows up early each Monday at a local coffee shop to review his sermon notes and consider how God wants him to apply what he heard. He wants to be a doer of God's Word. Dave takes listening and doing seriously.

WHAT IF YOU DIDN'T HAVE IT?

A good way to grow in your appreciation of something is to try to imagine life without it. Most of us wouldn't go into shock immediately if the Sunday gathering were taken away. We'd keep reading our Bibles. We'd keep listening to our Christian CDs. But what if you couldn't gather in a local church to worship? What if you were the only Christian in sight?

What if you *really* felt alone?

When I was fourteen, I was part of a gymnastics team that went to Sapporo, Japan, to compete. Because I'm half Japanese and it was the first time I'd traveled outside the country, I was thrilled. Each of us would be staying by ourselves overnight with a Japanese family. It sounded exciting, but I was just a kid. I definitely wasn't ready for the culture shock and sense of isolation that can come in a foreign country.

At the end of my first day apart from my English-speaking friends, I was overcome with intense loneliness. Even though I was surrounded by people, I had never felt so isolated. No one in the family could understand me, and I couldn't understand anyone. I was just a boy from Oregon feeling very, very out of place.

I'll never forget arriving at the gym the next day to be

reunited with my teammates. I had never been so excited to see other people *just like me*. Just to be near them was comforting. They knew me. They understood me. They were my team. We had the same home back in America.

I think something of what I experienced that reunion day in Japan should be present every time we walk into church. Through the gospel and participation in the local church, Christians are teammates in the deepest sense of the word. Our affection and love for God's people should be palpable. It should run deep. And our awareness of our need for others should fill us with an overwhelming sense of gratitude for the privilege of Sundays together.

Please don't take Sunday for granted. Do whatever it takes to rediscover the wonder of it all. Next Sunday, during the morning service, look around and remind yourself: *These are my blood-bought brothers and sisters in Christ. We are His church, His people. We are here this morning to proclaim His work in our lives. We are here to give witness to the world of His great love and power and glory.*

Every Sunday, the One who sought us and saved us from our sin extends an invitation to draw near to Him *together* through the work of His Son. He invites us to recapture the passion of Psalm 122:1, which says, "I was glad when they said to me, 'Let us go to the house of the LORD!'"

This Sunday, millions of Christians around the world will gather in the open air, in mud huts, in rented theaters, in homes, in elementary schools, in multimillion-dollar facilities. But the places we gather are of little consequence. What matters is the One we have come to worship and enjoy. What matters is that we will be together, with Him, on His day.

I hope you'll be there, too…with all your heart.

Chapter 7

THE DEAREST
PLACE ON EARTH

It's Time to Say Yes

Without a doubt, they were some of the most extraordinary days in history. Jesus had risen from the dead. Soon He would ascend to heaven. And during that interlude of days, Jesus kept appearing to His disciples to reassure them and to prepare them for their mission after His departure.

One morning, beside the Sea of Galilee, Jesus appeared in the mist along the shore (you remember the story, told on the last page of John's Gospel). He had come to help His friends catch a net-load of fish. He had come to serve them breakfast. But He had come for a much more important reason, too.

He still had to talk to Peter.

You know Peter. Everyone's favorite disciple. The guy with the most opinions and most mistakes to his credit. The bravest, boldest believer who…just didn't do commitment well.

And now Jesus had come to look him in the eye.

A CONVERSATION BETWEEN FRIENDS

I think Peter was quieter than usual that morning. Wouldn't you be if, only days before, you had angrily announced that you did *not*, did *not*, did *not* follow Jesus? I think Peter stood on that beach in the soft morning light wondering what he would see when he met Jesus' eye, wondering if anything—anything at all—could erase the stain of his awful denials.

But listen to the conversation John records…

"Simon, son of John," Jesus said, using Peter's formal name. "Do you love me more than these?"

Perhaps Peter glanced at the other disciples. Or maybe he was too ashamed to. After all, he had once boasted loudly of his loyalty only to have his resolve crumble in cowardice. Now he answered quietly. "Yes, Lord; you know that I love you."

"Feed my lambs," Jesus said.

With hardly a pause, He put the question to Peter again. "Simon, son of John, do you love me?"

Again Peter said, "Yes, Lord; you know that I love you."

Jesus replied, "Tend my sheep."

Then a third and final time, He asked the question. "Simon, son of John, do you love me?"

This time, John records, Peter was grieved. Did his eyes well up with tears? Did his emotions, always so close to the surface, spill out in exasperation? "Lord," he answered, "you know everything; you know that I love you."

And Jesus said to him, "Feed my sheep."

Don't you love the care of the Savior in this conversation between friends? Without reference to Peter's sin, Jesus led him through the steps of his repentance and restored him to his place alongside the other disciples. For three denials, three gentle questions. And for each question from Jesus, a heartfelt confession from Peter.

Now Peter was ready to put his love into action and reclaim his true calling—to care deeply about the flock of God.

You might be ready, too.

JESUS HAS SOMETHING
TO TELL YOU

Do you recognize yourself in Peter? I do. All the good intentions, all the botched follow-throughs. And I recognize the moment when Jesus astonishes me yet again with grace.

I think many of us church-daters are like Peter. We really do love Jesus; we just have trouble putting that love into action. It doesn't help that we're proud and enjoy our independence. The church and all that comes with it feels like baggage, like something that will slow us down. We're pretty sure we'd rather go it alone. Pretty sure, that is, until we make a mess of things. Then we stand trembling, waiting for Jesus, all our hopes hanging by a thread.

But here's what I want you to see: Jesus comes for us at moments like that. He knows that we love Him, and He wants us to know it, too. He has something to give us that we can't live without. And He has something important to tell us about our future.

If you passionately love Jesus Christ but haven't been committed to the church, I hope you've heard your Master come to you on the pages of this book. I hope you've heard Him speaking gently to you, like He did to Peter. I hope you've received His gracious forgiveness of your wrong attitudes toward the church. I hope you've heard your own spirit saying yes on every page—"Yes, I *do* love You, Lord. You know I do!"

Of one thing I'm certain—Jesus is not here to condemn. Instead, He asks you to do something very specific.

And it's not what you expect, is it? You *expect* Him to say, "Oh, you love Me? Then live an outstanding Christian life," or "Then evangelize the world," or "Then you should be communing with Me in private."

But instead He calls you to simply love His church. Because caring deeply about what Jesus cares about is your true calling.

Do you believe it? Are you ready to reclaim it? Loving what Jesus loves is always what matters most—whether you're an impulsive apostle named Peter, or a cautious man named Jack, or a young pastor named Josh.

A HEART FOR THE CHURCH

The months I've spent writing *Stop Dating the Church!* are leading up to my becoming the senior pastor of my church. The man whose place I'm stepping into is my dear friend and mentor in ministry, C. J. Mahaney.

Remember those tapes called *Passion for the Church* that first transformed my view of the church? It was C. J.

preaching those messages. Little did I know as I drove around listening to him that less than a year later I'd be packing up my car to move across the country so I could live in his basement and have him teach me how to be a pastor.

C. J. has been serving our church for twenty-seven years. Now he's passing that responsibility to me. He's in the prime of his life and ministry and could easily continue leading our church for years. But he wants to give me the chance to lead while I'm young—and while he's still around to counsel and encourage me.

When strangers find out I'm a pastor, they give me the most quizzical looks. "You don't look old enough to be a pastor," they say. I just smile. I know they assume that I must be the youth pastor, and I don't tell them otherwise. Besides, I feel silly saying I'm a "senior" pastor—there's nothing senior about me. People would think I must senior-pastor a church of preschoolers.

To say that I feel inadequate is an understatement. I joke with people that what I lack in wisdom I make up for with inexperience. The only reason I can step into the role is because I'm surrounded by older, more experienced pastors on my team, men who have served for many years, who are supporting me and seeking to assist me. This is humbling, but it's also an inspiring picture of what the church is supposed to be—not a place where people are jockeying for power, but where people willingly take whatever role best serves God's purpose.

And in the midst of my weakness, I also have faith and joy at the prospect of serving in my church. I love the people of Covenant Life. They're among the most humble and godly people I know. And I truly believe I was born to do this. That is, I view this as my life calling. I have no ambition or even desire for ministry apart from Covenant Life Church in Gaithersburg, Maryland. My work as a writer is secondary. A recent decision to stop traveling extensively and doing conferences was made without a twinge of regret. My heart is in my church. Acts 20:28 says Jesus bought the church with His own blood. How can I not give it my life?

That's what Peter did.

And we know what happened next. We just have to look over to the next page in our Bible to find out.

THIS IS OUR TIME

The next page of the Bible—Acts chapter 1—is the first page of church history. You and I trace our spiritual ancestry to that page. There, Jesus charges His followers with being His witnesses to the ends of the earth. Then He returns to heaven. A few paragraphs later, the mighty wind of the Spirit blows into a meeting of 120 waiting, expectant believers…and the church is born.

Peter, for one, is never the same. Want a profile of commitment to the church of Christ? Watch Peter and the rest of the apostles as they set off across the known world to spread the news of salvation in Christ. Every letter, every prayer to the last page of the New Testament, is proof that Peter and his friends *did* choose to love most what Jesus loved, and *did* tend His flock.

Consider the countless women and men since then—not great leaders or teachers or pastors, mind you, just ordinary believers—who have lived their lives for God's glory in local churches. How many do we know now by name? Hardly any. And yet their faithfulness to the Savior is directly connected to the fact that two thousand years later, you and I know Jesus. If they had not stood for the gospel in their generation, we wouldn't be here in ours. They lived out God's Word; they met in fellowship to give witness to the gospel; they proclaimed Christ crucified with their words and their lives.

Through them God saved and discipled the person who shared the Good News with another. Who witnessed to another, and another, and another—on and on through the generations till we come to the man or woman who shared the gospel of Jesus Christ with you and me.

And here we are.

This is our time.

Today, *we* are Christ's church (He continues to choose the foolish things of the world to shame the wise, doesn't He?).

Today, Jesus comes to us with the same question. Will you and I, He wants to know, commit to passing on through His church in this generation the treasure of His glorious gospel?

My brothers and sisters, it's time for us to say yes.

Charles Spurgeon once referred to the local church as "the dearest place on earth." You know, when I was a church-dater I just wouldn't have understood that sentiment.

But now I do.

NOTES

CHAPTER 1

George Barna—George Barna, "Number of Unchurched Adults Has Nearly Doubled Since 2001," *The Barna Group,* 4 May 2004.
http://www.barna.org/FlexPage.aspx?Page=BarnaUpdateNarrow &BarnaUpdateID=163 (accessed 1 June 2004).

Paul David Tripp—Paul David Tripp, *Instruments in the Redeemer's Hands* (Phillipsburg, NJ: P & R Publishing, 2002), 20–21.

CHAPTER 2

The opening of this chapter about my wedding is taken from the final chapter of my book *Boy Meets Girl* (Sisters, OR: Multnomah Publishers, 2000).

Eric Lane—G. Eric Lane, *I Want to Be a Church Member* (Bryntirion, Wales: Evangelical Press of Wales, 1992), 21.

Richard Phillips—Richard D. Phillips, *The Church* (Phillipsburg, NJ: P & R Publishing, 2004), 27.

John Stott—John R. W. Stott, *The Message of Ephesians* (Downers Grove, IL: InterVarsity Press, 1986).

CHAPTER 3

Chuck Colson—Chuck Colson and Ellen Vaughn, *Being the Body* (Nashville, TN: W Publishing Group, 2003), 271.

Charles Spurgeon—Charles Spurgeon, *Spurgeon at His Best,* comp. Tom Carter (Grand Rapids, MI: Baker, 1988), 33–34.

Brian Habig and Les Newsom—Brian Habig and Les Newsom, *The Enduring Community* (Jackson, MS: Reformed University Press, 2001), 173–74.

"New life…new society"—This phrase is drawn from John Stott's *The Message of Ephesians* (Downers Grove, IL: InterVarsity Press, 1986).

Donald Whitney—Donald Whitney, *Spiritual Disciplines Within the Church* (Chicago, IL: Moody, 1996), 81–82.

CHAPTER 4

John Stott—Stott, *The Message of Ephesians* commentary, 129.

John Loftness—John Loftness, *Why Small Groups?* (Gaithersburg, MD: Sovereign Grace Publishing, 1996), 21.

CHAPTER 5

Donald Whitney—Whitney, *Spiritual Disciplines Within the Church*, 66.

Charles Spurgeon—Charles Spurgeon, quoted in ibid., 67.

Menno Simons—Menno Simons, *The Complete Writings of Menno Simons,* ed. John C. Wenger (Scottdale, PA: Herald Press, 1956), 413.

CHAPTER 6

The idea for this chapter was suggested by C. J. Mahaney. And it was greatly influenced by messages that both C. J. and Jeff Purswell gave on the same subject.

Matthew Henry—Matthew Henry, quoted in *A Quest for Godliness* by J. I. Packer (Wheaton, IL: Crossway Books, 1990), 239.

Ibid., 240.

John Piper—John Piper, from a sermon titled "Take Care How You Listen! Part Two," delivered on 22 February 1998.

http://www.desiringgod.org/library/sermons/98/022298.html
(accessed 21 May 2004).

J. I. Packer—J. I. Packer, quoted in Donald Whitney,
Spiritual Disciplines within the Church, 69, originally from *The
Preacher and Preaching.*

Donald Whitney—Whitney, *Spiritual Disciplines Within the
Church,* 69.

John Piper—John Piper, from "Take Care How You Listen!
Part Two," 22 February 1998 (accessed 21 May 2004).

Recommended Reading

Knowing God
by J. I. Packer (Downers Grove, IL: InterVarsity, 1993). A classic book that gives basic yet transforming guidance on being a Christian.

Spiritual Disciplines Within the Church
by Donald S. Whitney (Chicago: Moody Publishers, 1996). This book will give you in-depth direction for your participation in the local church.

9 Marks of a Healthy Church
by Mark Dever (Wheaton, IL: Crossway Books, 1997). Highly recommended for pastors and leaders. A book that will teach you the qualities that matter most in a local church.

The Cross and Christian Ministry
by D. A. Carson (Grand Rapids, MI: Baker Book House, 2004). This short book defines Christian ministry in light of Christ's work on the cross. A must-have book for understanding the focus, content, and nature of all effective ministry. Highly recommended, especially for leaders.

The Cross Centered Life
by C. J. Mahaney (Sisters, OR: Multnomah Publishers, 2002).

A book that clearly and succinctly explains what it means to center your life around the gospel.

Bible Doctrine

by Wayne Grudem (Grand Rapids, MI: Zondervan, 1999). A very accessible systematic theology that will help you define your own doctrinal convictions.

Instruments in the Redeemer's Hands

by Paul David Tripp (Phillipsburg, NJ: P & R Press, 2002). This book will equip you to understand how God works through individuals in the local church to apply God's Word and bring about change. It will serve anyone who desires to be an effective counselor to others and experience personal growth in godliness.

Evangelical Feminism and Biblical Truth

by Wayne Grudem (Sisters, OR: Multnomah Publishers, 2004). Available late 2004. If you're wrestling with questions about male-female roles in marriage as well as the church, this thorough and masterful book is essential reading for laypeople and pastors alike.

Feminine Appeal

by Carolyn Mahaney (Wheaton, IL: Crossway, 2003). An outstanding book that helps women live out the instruction of Titus 2.

ACKNOWLEDGMENTS

A special thanks...

To Don Jacobson, Kevin Marks, and Doug Gabbert for their enthusiasm for this book and their care for me and my family.

To all the men and women who e-mailed me their stories and talked so honestly about their experiences with the church.

To all the pastors at Covenant Life, who supported me while I wrote. My particular thanks to Grant and Kenneth, who uniquely shoulder the responsibilities of leadership with me. To the members of my church, who sustained me with their prayers. I can't believe I get to serve as your pastor.

To Jeff Purswell, Brian Chesemore, and my dad, Gregg, for reading the book and giving me feedback. To Mark Dever and his team of pastors, who gave me invaluable critique and encouragement. To Justin Taylor for helping me track down quotes.

To David and Heather Kopp, who served as my editors. They owned the message of this book. Without their partnership throughout this project it simply would not exist. David helped me plot the outline. Heather guided me through revisions. Then David polished like only he can. I want to specifically thank David for proposing the story of Peter and Jesus in the last chapter and for reworking my attempts into something worthwhile. This husband-wife team is, in my humble opinion, the best editing team in the world. And to Jennifer Gott, who did the line edit.

To C. J. Mahaney. I dedicated this book to you because without you I never would have stopped dating the church myself. Thank you for loving the Savior and His church. Thank you for setting an example for me to follow. And thanks for trusting me with the church you love so dearly.

To Joshua Quinn and Emma, for running into my office each morning to interrupt me and hug me. You bring so much joy to your daddy's heart.

To *my* bride, Shannon. She believed in this book on the days I was ready to give up. She encouraged me, cheered me on, and joyfully shouldered the sacrifice involved with having a husband writing. Shannon, you are a gift I don't deserve. I love you so much. I want to love you like Jesus loves the Church.

To my wonderful Savior, Jesus Christ, who not only rescued me from the wrath I deserve but gave me the privilege of serving as a pastor. My prayer is that this book will strengthen and encourage Your Church.

ABOUT THE AUTHOR

 Joshua Harris got his start in writing as the editor of *New Attitude*, a Christian magazine for homeschool teens. He wrote his first book, *I Kissed Dating Goodbye,* at age twenty-one. In it he challenged teenagers to enjoy the opportunities of singleness and wait on romance till they were ready for commitment. The surprise success of the book led to new opportunities, including media appearances, a popular conference tour, and the three-part *I Kissed Dating Goodbye Video Series.*

In 1997, Joshua moved from Oregon to Gaithersburg, Maryland, to be trained for pastoral ministry at Covenant Life Church. It was there—five years after giving up the dating game himself—that Joshua met, courted, and married his bride, Shannon.

In his second book, *Boy Meets Girl: Say Hello to Courtship,* Joshua shared their love story and the lessons God taught them. The highly anticipated sequel provided practical guidance for couples on issues like communication, the role of family and friends in courtship, dealing with past sexual sin, and questions to ask before engagement.

Joshua's third book, *Not Even a Hint,* tackled the common challenges of sexual temptation. Written for both men and women, it gives a practical, grace-centered plan for defeating lust and celebrating purity. The book's honesty and vulnerability won many new readers, particularly those who had been skeptical of Joshua's books on dating.

In the fall of 2004, Joshua assumed the role of senior pastor at Covenant Life Church. He and Shannon have two children, Emma and Joshua Quinn.

For information about Josh's work, online sermons, and stories from readers, visit his website at:

www.joshharris.com

www.covlife.org

Feel free to contact Josh. Though he can't respond personally to all correspondence, he'd love to get your feedback.

Joshua Harris

P.O. Box 249

Gaithersburg, MD 20884-0249

jharris@covlife.org

Your sexuality is not the enemy...lust is.

1-59052-147-1

Lust wants to twist your natural sexual desires into something destructive. God can free you to live in purity and true joy. He calls us to "not even a hint" of sexual immorality—and gives us everything we need to obey.

This refreshingly honest and hope-filled book helps men and women face the daily reality of sexual temptation. Forthright without being graphic, it covers topics like entertainment and media, how to use Scripture to fight the lies of lust, and how Christians should deal with masturbation.

Practical and centered on God's grace, this book will guide you in creating your own "custom tailored" plan of resisting lust and celebrating purity.

Individual study guides for men and women can help your small group go further on the path of holiness. Each features discussion guides and questions for each chapter. The women's edition features reflections from Shannon and helpful tips on modesty.

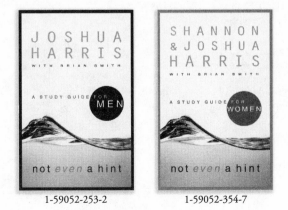

1-59052-253-2   1-59052-354-7

Isn't it time to rethink dating?

I KISSED DATING GOODBYE

Dating. Isn't there a better way? Reorder your romantic life in the light of God's Word and find more fulfillment than the dating game could ever give—a life of purposeful singleness.

ISBN 1-59052-135-8

I KISSED DATING GOODBYE VIDEO SERIES

Three-video series   ISBN 1-59052-180-3

Video-Part 1: Love   ISBN 1-59052-212-5

Video-Part 2: Purity   ISBN 1-59052-213-3

Video-Part 3: Trust   ISBN 1-59052-214-1

I KISSED DATING GOODBYE STUDY GUIDE

The *I Kissed Dating Goodbye Study Guide*, based on Joshua Harris's phenomenal best-seller, provides youth with a new resource for living a lifestyle of sincere love, true purity, and purposeful singleness.

ISBN 1-59052-136-6

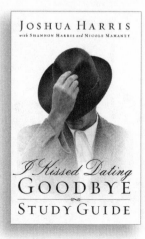

Perfect for Couples

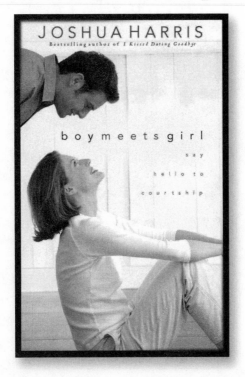

Boy Meets Girl is the perfect book to help focus your relationship on God. It helps couples journey from friendship to marriage while avoiding the pitfalls of today's often directionless relationships. It gives practical advice about communication, involving your family in your relationship, keeping your relationship pure, dealing with past sexual sin, and the questions to ask before you get engaged.

ISBN 1-57673-709-8